OPPOSING
VIEWPOINTS®
SERIES

Ethics

Other Books of Related Interest:

Opposing Viewpoints Series

Abortion

Democracy

Cloning

The Environment

Euthanasia

Genetic Engineering

Mass Media

Social Issues

Current Controversies Series

The Abortion Controversy

Assisted Suicide

Conserving the Environment

Medical Ethics

At Issue Series

The Ethics of Abortion

The Ethics of Capital Punishment

The Ethics of Euthanasia

The Ethics of Genetic Engineering

The Ethics of Human Cloning

Human Embryo Experimentation

Physician-Assisted Suicide

"Congress shall make
no law . . . abridging
the freedom of speech,
or of the press."

First Amendment to the U.S. Constitution

The basic foundation of our democracy is the First Amendment guarantee of freedom of expression. The Opposing Viewpoints Series is dedicated to the concept of this basic freedom and the idea that it is more important to practice it than to enshrine it.

Ethics

Laurie diMauro and Tina Grant, Book Editors

GREENHAVEN PRESS
An imprint of Thomson Gale, a part of The Thomson Corporation

Detroit • New York • San Francisco • San Diego • New Haven, Conn.
Waterville, Maine • London • Munich

Bonnie Szumski, *Publisher*
Helen Cothran, *Managing Editor*

For more information, contact:
Greenhaven Press
27500 Drake Rd.
Farmington Hills, MI 48331-3535
Or you can visit our Internet site at http://www.gale.com

LIBRARY OF CONGRESS CATALOGING-IN-PUBLICATION DATA

Ethics / Laurie diMauro and Tina Grant, book editors
    p. cm. -- (Opposing viewpoints)
    Includes bibliographical references and index.
    0-7377-3319-5 (lib. : alk. paper) 0-7377-3320-9 (pbk. : alk. paper)
    1. Ethics. I. DiMauro, Laurie. II. Grant, Tina. III. Opposing viewpoints
series (Unnumbered)
    BJ21.E84 2006
    170--dc22
                                                    2006041179

Printed in the United States of America
10 9 8 7 6 5 4 3 2 1

Contents

Chapter Three: Are Modern Biomedical Practices Ethical?

Chapter Four: Are American Corporations Ethical?

Why Consider
Opposing Viewpoints?

> *"The only way in which a human being can make some approach to knowing the whole of a subject is by hearing what can be said about it by persons of every variety of opinion and studying all modes in which it can be looked at by every character of mind. No wise man ever acquired his wisdom in any mode but this."*
>
> *John Stuart Mill*

In our media-intensive culture it is not difficult to find differing opinions. Thousands of newspapers and magazines and dozens of radio and television talk shows resound with differing points of view. The difficulty lies in deciding which opinion to agree with and which "experts" seem the most credible. The more inundated we become with differing opinions and claims, the more essential it is to hone critical reading and thinking skills to evaluate these ideas. Opposing Viewpoints books address this problem directly by presenting stimulating debates that can be used to enhance and teach these skills. The varied opinions contained in each book examine many different aspects of a single issue. While examining these conveniently edited opposing views, readers can develop critical thinking skills such as the ability to compare and contrast authors' credibility, facts, argumentation styles, use of persuasive techniques, and other stylistic tools. In short, the Opposing Viewpoints Series is an ideal way to attain the higher-level thinking and reading skills so essential in a culture of diverse and contradictory opinions.

In addition to providing a tool for critical thinking, Opposing Viewpoints books challenge readers to question their own strongly held opinions and assumptions. Most people form their opinions on the basis of upbringing, peer pressure, and personal, cultural, or professional bias. By reading carefully balanced opposing views, readers must directly confront new ideas as well as the opinions of those with whom they disagree. This is not to simplistically argue that everyone who reads opposing views will—or should—change his or her opinion. Instead, the series enhances readers' understanding of their own views by encouraging confrontation with opposing ideas. Careful examination of others' views can lead to the readers' understanding of the logical inconsistencies in their own opinions, perspective on why they hold an opinion, and the consideration of the possibility that their opinion requires further evaluation.

Evaluating Other Opinions

To ensure that this type of examination occurs, Opposing Viewpoints books present all types of opinions. Prominent spokespeople on different sides of each issue as well as well-known professionals from many disciplines challenge the reader. An additional goal of the series is to provide a forum for other, less known, or even unpopular viewpoints. The opinion of an ordinary person who has had to make the decision to cut off life support from a terminally ill relative, for example, may be just as valuable and provide just as much insight as a medical ethicist's professional opinion. The editors have two additional purposes in including these less known views. One, the editors encourage readers to respect others' opinions—even when not enhanced by professional credibility. It is only by reading or listening to and objectively evaluating others' ideas that one can determine whether they are worthy of consideration. Two, the inclusion of such viewpoints encourages the important critical thinking skill of objectively evaluating an author's credentials and bias. This evaluation will illuminate an author's reasons for taking a particular stance on an issue and will aid in readers' evaluation of the author's ideas.

It is our hope that these books will give readers a deeper understanding of the issues debated and an appreciation of the complexity of even seemingly simple issues when good and honest people disagree. This awareness is particularly important in a democratic society such as ours in which people enter into public debate to determine the common good. Those with whom one disagrees should not be regarded as enemies but rather as people whose views deserve careful examination and may shed light on one's own.

Thomas Jefferson once said that "difference of opinion leads to inquiry, and inquiry to truth." Jefferson, a broadly educated man, argued that "if a nation expects to be ignorant and free . . . it expects what never was and never will be." As individuals and as a nation, it is imperative that we consider the opinions of others and examine them with skill and discernment. The Opposing Viewpoints Series is intended to help readers achieve this goal.

David L. Bender and Bruno Leone,
Founders

Introduction

"Let us then be what we are, and speak what we think, and in all things keep ourselves loyal to truth."
—Henry Wadsworth Longfellow

Ethics, also known as moral philosophy, attempts to define what is right and what is wrong in human behavior. People engaging in ethical reasoning are trying to discover how they and others should act. Many individuals look to religious teachings to guide them in their ethical decisions. Others use logic in an attempt to discover how certain actions may benefit or harm themselves and society. To some degree, then, ethics is the purview of individuals, who must struggle with their consciences to make moral decisions. However, societies also must engage in ethical decision making, and most have a core set of values that they use to guide them in making policies that benefit the nation as a whole. Americans, for example, have long valued freedom, equality, and justice, what many philosophers consider the cornerstones of democracy. Free societies also value honesty, without which societies cease to function. Examining how important an ethical concept such as honesty is to America can help show how vital ethics are to all societies.

Without honesty, the essential mechanisms of society break down. Even the most basic commercial transactions depend on the integrity of those involved. For example, when Americans purchase a new car, they are entrusting their lives to the automobile's manufacturer, who has assured them that the car will run safely. If consumers did not trust car manufacturers to make safe products, they would not purchase them. Another area where honesty is essential is in the political process.

Fair elections are impossible without honesty, for example. Certainly no one would bother voting if they believed that their ballots would simply be altered to benefit the party in power. Court proceedings, as well, depend on witnesses who swear "to tell the truth, the whole truth, and nothing but the truth." Relationships between family members and friends also depend upon honesty. Spouses who lie about extramarital affairs are often served with divorce papers, for instance, because dishonesty damages the trust essential to marriage.

Despite the importance of honesty, scandals involving dishonesty have affected nearly every facet of American life. Dishonesty in the political sphere has garnered the most attention. When President Richard Nixon resigned in 1974 after it was discovered that he had lied about his knowledge of the break-in at the Democratic National Headquarters in the Watergate complex in June 1972, repercussions were registered throughout politics and American society. Americans reasoned that if the president himself would lie and cheat, then the federal government could not be trusted. Recent political scandals involving congressional representatives have further weakened the public's trust in government. For instance, Representative Randy "Duke" Cunningham was indicted in 2005 for taking bribes from defense contractor Jack Abramoff.

In business, too, dishonesty has undermined Americans' faith in the nation's commitment to ethics. For decades the tobacco industry hid the dangers of smoking, arguing—despite scientists' claims to the contrary—that cigarettes were not harmful. Only when forced to by lawsuits did the industry begin to come clean about the adverse health effects of its products. In recent years leaders of corporations such as Enron and WorldCom have lied about company finances and cheated their employees and shareholders. The pharmaceutical company Merck failed to disclose the risk of heart disease associated with its Vioxx pain medication and may be responsible for thousands of deaths as a result. Some believe incidents such as these reveal corruption at the core of American business.

Many Americans also believe that dishonesty is endemic among U.S. citizens. For example, among more than twenty-four thousand high school students surveyed by the Los Angeles–based Josephson Institute of Ethics in 2004, nearly two-thirds reported that they had cheated on a test and one-quarter said they had stolen from a store during the previous twelve months. The survey revealed a startling degree of dishonesty among teenagers both at school and in their personal lives: Eighty-two percent admitted that within the past year they had lied to a parent about something significant, and 83 percent had copied someone else's homework. Four out of ten students reported that they "sometimes lie to save money," and more than half of the boys (52 percent) and a third of the girls (32 percent) agreed that "a person has to lie or cheat sometimes in order to succeed." Yet 92 percent of the survey respondents indicated that they were satisfied with their own ethics and character.

The disjunction between youths' view of themselves as good people and their actual behavior calls into question the notion that Americans agree on and value a core set of values. If dishonesty is indeed becoming more prevalent, the transactions and relationships that are central to a free society could be in jeopardy. The authors in *Opposing Viewpoints: Ethics* examine the issue of honesty and other controversies concerning ethics in the following chapters: What Motivates People to Behave Ethically? Why Should People Behave Ethically? Are Modern Biomedical Practices Ethical? Are American Corporations Ethical? The ethical issues debated in this book have a significant impact on every individual and society in the world.

What Motivates People to Behave Ethically?

Chapter Preface

While virtually everyone believes that people should act in an ethical manner, understanding what motivates people to behave ethically can be difficult. One theory is that people behave morally because of belief in God. Another theory is that human biology dictates that people behave ethically. A final theory holds that ethical behavior is a natural consequence of social living.

Many ethical systems have a religious basis, holding that belief in God and comprehension of the relationship between God and humanity provides the foundation for moral behavior. Adherents to the Judeo-Christian tradition look to the biblical commandments as the basis for correct conduct in the hope of gaining the eternal reward of heaven. Adherents to other religious traditions similarly refer to holy texts and teachings for guidance in interpreting contemporary moral dilemmas. These people are motivated both by fear of punishment and hope of reward. For example, Christians may avoid adultery because they do not want to risk being punished by God or ruin their chances of getting into heaven.

Some ethical systems look to human nature itself for motivation, arguing that because people are rational creatures they can be energized to act morally by reason. Modern science, without reference to a supreme or supernatural being, locates the underlying motivation for ethical behavior in human biology, theorizing that people consider the social consequences of certain actions to formulate how best to act in the future. If a particular act—murder, for example—is found to adversely affect society, then the society forbids it. If society is protected in this way, these theorists postulate, then the individuals living within it will be protected as well. Thus, behaving ethically is biologically advantageous for the individual, who depends on society for his or her well-being.

Another theory holds that people are impelled to act ethically simply because others in their society do so. When faced with difficult decisions, this theory postulates, people tend to make choices based on what others do in similar situations. When faced with a decision about whether or not to cheat on an exam, for example, a student may wonder whether his or her peers have ever cheated on a test. If the student's friends have largely avoided cheating, the student is likely to as well, these theorists claim.

Many commentators believe that each of these theories has merit. According to them, people can be motivated to goodness by many different means—whether by religion, biology, or society. It is notable that even in the face of evil, people still believe in humanity's capacity to act ethically. In the midst of the Nazi Holocaust, diarist Anne Frank affirmed, "In spite of everything, I still believe that people are really good at heart." It would seem that the motivation to behave morally, no matter its origin, is strong. In the following chapter authors discuss the underlying assumptions that ground modern ethical systems. Their views provide insight into why ethical behavior is the cornerstone of human societies.

*"If there were no God, there would be
no morality, because nothing would be
intrinsically right or wrong."*

Belief in God Motivates
People to Behave Ethically

Lewis B. Smedes

*Lewis B. Smedes was an evangelical Protestant minister who
served as chair of the Department of Philosophy and Ethics at
Fuller Theological Seminary in Pasadena, California, until his
retirement in 1995. He died in 2002. In the following viewpoint,
excerpted from his spiritual memoir* My God & I, *Smedes argues
that belief in God provides the foundation for moral behavior.
He contends that without God, nothing would be intrinsically
wrong or right. Smedes also maintains that the biblical commandments provide guidance for making difficult moral decisions but that listening to others who see reality differently can
help one determine what is right and wrong.*

As you read, consider the following questions:

1. What role does Smedes assign to God in the development of morality?
2. How do the teachings of Jesus influence the author's
   understanding of moral law?
3. How does Smedes define moral discernment?

When I arrived at Fuller in 1968, the teacher of Christian ethics was a man in his mid-thirties with the electric eyes of a recent convert, which he was—not from the world to Christ, but from Christ back to the world. Jaymes Morgan had the magnetic makings of a new breed of evangelical leader in a tumultuous time. But he had cancer, had had it for some months before I came on the scene, and he died hardly more than a year after I arrived.

Getting into Ethics

Morgan's death left us with a big hole in the curriculum. I was by this time a tenured faculty member still learning how to teach the philosophy of religion—which deals with such things as how a powerful and good God could let the world get into the mess it seems always to be in.

Now we needed someone to teach ethics—which deals with how weak and sinful human beings can know what is right and what is good. But evangelicals with scholarly credentials to teach ethics were rare at that time. We looked everywhere and found no one to match our needs. During one more futile meeting of our search committee, and after thinking about it for no longer than thirty seconds, I offered myself for the job. I proposed that we look for candidates in both the philosophy of religion and in ethics; if we found a philosopher before we found an ethicist, I would switch over to ethics. A generous offer, I thought; others were probably more impressed by my presumption!

The next thing we knew we had found a fine philosopher of religion, and there I was, at fifty, leaping into a complex and controversial subject for which I had few academic qualifications to recommend me. I did not have the time to make myself over into the sort of bona fide scholar who writes articles in academic journals and gives learned lectures at conferences. But I might be able, I thought, to teach future ministers how to guide their people through the moral quandaries of life.

When we talk about ethics in a theological seminary, we mean to be talking about what God requires of us and how we can know it. And since this memoir is, strictly speaking, about my walk with God and not about ethics, I will limit myself to three assumptions that I have made about God in our efforts to learn his will for the moral choices we are called on to make.

Basic Assumptions

I assumed, first of all, that God the Father is the origin of all morality. If there were no God, there would be no morality, because nothing would be intrinsically right or wrong. Without God, we would probably create social conventions and social rules that might keep people from putting their hands on our purses or around our throats. But this is self-protection born of self-interest, and, while it may be practical, it does not have much to do with what is not morally right and morally wrong.

With God, we are called to act not in self-interest but in obedience to his moral law. The fact, however, is that obeying his moral law leads us to what is in the best interests of all of us. A rational God who would go to the trouble of creating a world full of free-willed people must, I thought, have a design in mind for how these people could best live together. God's design is what makes things right or wrong. We do right if we live according to his design. We do wrong when we violate his design. So what we call moral law—or the divine commandments—is a manual for life at its best.

Much of the time, if our hearts are pure, the commandments are all we need to live a good moral life. We know that when we talk, we must be truthful. When we make a promise, we must keep it. When we want something our neighbor has, we must keep our hands off of it. When our neighbor does us wrong, we must not kill him for revenge. And no matter how unhappy our marriages may be, we must be faithful to them. Thus, for most of our daily moral choices, we do not need to study ethics; all we need is a knowledge of God's commandments and a will to obey them.

But much of the time is not all of the time. No doubt corporate CEOs who lie to their shareholders and politicians who lie to their public know and believe intellectually that lying is immoral. Why then do they lie? They lie to others because they first lie to themselves. The lies we tell ourselves are the most subtle of all lies. Nobody wakes up in the morning and says to himself, "I think I shall lie to myself today."

The deception happens in such a tiny fraction of a second that the self-deceiver is not even aware that he has lied to himself. What lies does he tell himself? One of them is the lie that he is not really lying when he tells a lie. Another is the lie that the moral law does not apply to him, at least not in this case. In short, people tell bold-faced lies about very important things, and feel no guilt about their lying because they lie to themselves about what they are doing. Their problem is not with their heads, but with their hearts.

The Second and Third Assumptions

My second assumption was about God the Son. I did not assume that Jesus Christ brought us a new ethic to replace the old one. I assumed that he showed us two new ways of understanding the old one. The first has to do with what: [It] showed us that if we have love, we will do *more* than just saying no to what the commandments forbid. The second with how: he showed us how to obey the moral law in a way that helps other people. Jesus' way of love, then, calls for doing *more* than saying no to bad things, and it is the way of doing good things in ways that are helpful to other people.

Steiner. © 1997 by News World Communications, Inc. Reproduced by permission of *The Washington Times.*

My third assumption was about God the Spirit. The Spirit of God is our eye-opener to the human situation that requires a decision from us. The moral law by itself is not enough to guide us. What we need is the ability to see what is really going on in the human circumstances to which we are trying to apply the moral law.

We must remember, however, that the Spirit is not like an eye surgeon; he does not remove our cataracts. Nor is the Spirit like an optometrist; he does not prescribe new lenses for our eyeglasses. The Spirit works on what lies behind our eyes. It is said that what we see lies eighty percent behind our eyes. It is that eighty percent that the Spirit works on.

Ordinarily, we see what we want to see. We do not see what we do not want to see. We do not want to see reality, because we are afraid of what it might tell us. The Spirit, however, gives us courage and honesty to want to see the truth no matter how much we fear it. This is how the Spirit opens our eyes to reality: he takes the blinders of fear away.

Reality and Discernment

Seeing reality for what it is is what we call discernment. The work of discernment is very hard. Reality is always deucedly complicated; any human situation has far more to it than first meets anybody's eye. No one has twenty-twenty discernment. This is why we need other people to tell us what they see in the same chunk of reality that we are looking at. This is why people of the church need to share their visions of reality *with* each other before they shout their judgments at each other.

Teaching seminary students, I often used real-life situations about which someone had to make an important moral choice. Each student was given a written report of the situation. Invariably, some students protested: "Why do we need even to discuss it?" they said. "What is going on in this situation is perfectly obvious." But we did need to discuss it. Invariably, the students who thought that what was going on was as clear and as simple as the bark on a tree were shocked to learn that others, as smart and as spiritual as they were, were seeing things that they missed. It is always this way: discovering God's will for a human situation requires us to listen to what other people see in that situation.

I discovered a long time ago that listening to people who see reality differently than we do is one of the most important parts of discovering the will of God for that reality. Nobody sees reality whole; we all need others to show us the parts of it that they see better than we do. Nobody sees reality with total accuracy; we all need others to correct our own vision. This is why we need to pray for patience to see what is really going on before we decide what God wants us to do about it.

Consider what it was that opened Christian people's eyes to the fact that slavery was an evil thing. They had grown up listening to preachers who quoted passage after passage from the Bible to prove that slavery was not only the will of God, but was a blessing to both the slaves and their masters. What persuaded them that the preachers were wrong? What persuaded them that slavery was a curse to both masters and slaves?

It was not a scholar's new interpretation of Bible texts. The conversion came only when their eyes were finally opened to see slaves for what they were: members of the same human family as the masters who owned them, fellow human beings who, like them, wept when they grieved and laughed when they were happy, who aspired to better things for their children, and were as likely as any Calvinist to love the Lord their God. It took courage for people to see what they were afraid to see and hear what they did not want to hear.

Making Decisions

During most of my years at Fuller Seminary I served on the Bioethics Committee of the Huntington Memorial Hospital, one of the larger hospitals in the Los Angeles area. The task of this committee is to advise physicians on the moral aspects of the life-and-death medical decisions they are called on to make. We had to begin with the facts of the case. The facts of any case, however, range well beyond the facts that the doctor writes on the patient's chart. The facts of the case include facts about the desires of the family of the patient, about the patient's religious beliefs, about the civil law, and about the likely consequences that a given course of action would have on still others.

Once a pediatric surgeon came to us with this problem. A woman who had recently arrived from mainland China, the mother of a three-year-old boy, was living in an apartment in Los Angeles while she waited for her husband to join her. She neither spoke nor understood English. One afternoon while she was talking to someone on the phone, her son toddled out of the apartment and went outside. When she put down the phone, she called to him but he did not answer. She rushed in panic to the recreational area where the swimming pool was. There she found her son lying face down in the pool.

The manager of the apartment called 911 and the boy was rushed to the hospital. His brain, the thinking part of it, was already dead, though he was still breathing. But there were other serious complications. The doctor called in a translator who relayed his words in Chinese to the mother.

Here is the gist of what he told her: "Your little boy needs immediate surgery to stay alive. But if we do surgery and 'save' his 'life' he will exist on a respirator as a breathing vegetable for the rest of his life." He told the woman that she was the only person who could decide whether to operate or not.

But this woman did not have the slightest idea of how to go about making a decision; she had grown up in communist China and, as a woman, had never been allowed to make a major decision in all her life. She was paralyzed by the fear of her husband's wrath should he come home to a dead son. Through a translator, she told the doctor that she wanted him to decide what to do. He told her that he could not make the decision for her; only she could decide.

What was the right thing for the doctor to do? I did not know of a single biblical command that told me in so many words what God wanted him to do. What we needed was more than the divine law; we needed human wisdom. I remember that what we suggested for the doctor to consider (no ethics committee decides for a doctor) was this: we suggested that he tell the mother that he will do nothing for one week and that if she has no answer by then he would interpret her silence as a decision not to operate and to take her son off the respirator. I do not know what he did.

The Role of Love

It is seldom enough that we know *what* we should do. We also need to sense *the right way* to do it. This is where love must do its work. Take our duty to tell the truth, for instance. Without love, we are likely to spout the truth with no regard for its effect on the person to whom we tell it. But if we have love, or empathy, we can put ourselves in the other person's shoes, and this will give us a better chance of seeing the right time and the right way to tell her the truth.

I cannot remember ever having told my children a lie. But I do remember times when I told them the truth at the wrong time and, what is worse, in the wrong way. And I know that telling them the truth at the wrong time and in the wrong way often hurt them worse than if I had told a merciful lie.

How do we know the right time and the right way to tell the truth? How do we know when and how to tell a person that she is dying, or that her son has gotten himself in jail, or that her husband has lost his job, or that she has made a fool of herself, or that her little child has an incurable disease, or that his wife is having an affair? What we need more than anything else is the Spirit of love to open our eyes and ears to see and hear what is really going on in the heart and mind of the person to whom we are talking.

"Biological processes lead to the formation of . . . our 'moral sensibilities.'"

Biology Motivates People to Behave Ethically

Donald W. Murphy

Donald W. Murphy, who trained as a geneticist before leaving graduate studies to work as a park ranger, is a deputy director within the U.S. National Park System. In the following viewpoint he asserts that feedback about previous ethical actions helps individuals and societies make decisions about how to act in the future. When certain actions are seen to produce negative consequences, Murphy argues, people create rules to forbid such actions. These rules, which become a society's ethical code, help ensure the survival of humanity, he contends.

As you read, consider the following questions:

1. What does Murphy say is the basis for the biological approach to ethics?

2. As explained by the author, what difficulties are encountered in an ethical system that relies on feedback information?

3. What does Murphy say is the relationship between biological evolution and ethics?

T he thesis I propose here is simple. Morality and ethics should serve as the basis for public policy; and biological processes lead to the formation of what E. O. Wilson [in *Consilience: The Unity of Knowledge*] calls our "moral sensibilities." In other words, our notion of right and wrong naturally proceed from our biological evolution. Anything with which a consequence is associated also has an ethical component. This is most easily seen in three superordinate reference points that guide human behavior: (1) concern for individual survival; (2) concern for the survival of the entire culture; and (3) abstract or transcendent concerns that enhance the quality of life. We now understand that our individual survival, the survival of the culture as a whole, and our transcendent concerns are all inextricably bound to the survival of our planet from which we evolved or, more completely, the universe from which we evolved.

These reference points that guide human behavior have associated with them a set of rules, moral principles and rights and wrongs that modify human behavior to insure that these reference points are sustained. Most of the time when we speak of ethics or morals it is understood by most to be in a religious context or in the context of some personal and subjective value system. The point of my brief introduction to bioevolutionary ethics is to establish that there is another alternative, one that is objective and rooted in an understanding of our bioevolution.

This notion is not new. There are whole schools of thought and philosophy on the subject of ethics based in biology, particularly biological feedback loops. I hasten to add here that the assertion that ethics have evolved from our biological evolution has come and gone over the years and has been refuted by philosophical arguments rooted in David Hume's is/ought dichotomy [in *A Treatise or Human Nature*] and G.E. Moore's naturalistic fallacy [in *Principia Ethica*]. There has, in the past, been an inability on the part of evolutionary biologists to show the link between actions that promote survival and moral behavior. Since this is only a brief comment, I will not take the time to present counter arguments to these problems but will simply say that they are problems of language and the logical construct and no longer are valid.

Returning now to biological evolution, an often-cited example to make this point is that there is a moral or religious reason to abstain from alcohol. However, the alternative view is that society has observed the negative consequences that overindulgence in alcohol brings, and it has developed a set of rules to govern its consumption. Is it immoral to drink and drive, or deleterious to society as a whole and therefore wrong? Or are they one and the same?

The Basis for the Biological Approach

The basis for the biological approach to right and wrong is rooted in feedback information given to all biological organisms to enhance survivability through modification of behavior. The human brain is the most efficient processor of information known, and it is, of course, biological.

Most people are aware that our planet was threatened by our use of fluorocarbons. We were given the feedback that, if the use of these chemicals continued, our survival would be in jeopardy. Thus, we modified our behavior accordingly.

The following story helps illustrate the point about moral intolerance versus biologically-based right and wrong. I lived with the Mennonites in Belize for a time and lived amongst a very strict sect that believed the use of "modernisms," as they called them, was forbidden. They firmly held that the use of the internal combustion engine, chemicals, and such would eventually lead to the destruction of human kind and were therefore evil. Biologically-based ethics, on the other hand, would say that these Mennonites had enough cumulative experience to know that the nature of man was such that he would extract as much immediate advantage and gratification as possible from these new technological tools. Lacking wisdom, he would use the tools, blind of any negative consequences, and this would finally lead to his destruction. Therefore, it was necessary to make a series of rules to prevent this destruction, and, here, this was to be achieved by the restrictions against all "modernisms." For the biologist, this demonstrates a direct link between actions leading to survivability and morality.

A Uniform Approach to Ethics

It is my assertion that a more uniform approach to ethics is one based on our understanding of our biological evolution. Our social constructs, which are made up of a number of rules, laws, and principles, evolved as our minds developed through the eons. The human mind, provided with information, began to use this information to formulate rules that modified human behavior and would serve to increase the survivability of the species.

The policies that we develop in government should be a continuously refined set of rules that sustain the superordinate reference points mentioned earlier, the simplest of which is the concern for individual survival, followed by the concern for the survival of society. We will leave the concern for the transcendent aside for the moment. But here is the rub, or perhaps the irony. As we have become more sophisticated in collecting and processing information, we agree less and less on the meaning of that information. Instead of efficiently using the information we receive as a feedback process to modify behavior, we often find it difficult to agree on the interpretation of the information. While I will not go into all of the reasons for this, I will spend a few moments on some of the reasons for this quandary within the context of environmental policy.

The current administration [of George W. Bush], of which I am a member, has made it clear that it wants to use objective science as a basis for making decisions and developing policy. In the highly charged political atmosphere in which we work, this is easier said than done. Scientific information is often challenged when it does not conform to established social rules, norms, ideas, or laws that may have been originally designed to protect society. New information is considered suspect if it challenges previous information, and change is resisted until clear proof is established. Scientific information is supposed to be objective and unbiased. However, what we are often dealing with is not unbiased, clear scientific information with solid experimental proof behind it; rather we are dealing with scientific data that has been collected but is yet unproven. This often leads to vehement disagreements about the interpretation of information.

Then there is raw politics, ensuing from individual special interest or group special interest. In this context, information is interpreted in such a way as to protect the interest and, ostensibly, the survivability of an individual or group of individuals. Conflicts result, and, instead of being used as an objective tool to formulate policy or make decisions about what is right and wrong, information becomes fodder for acrimonious debate.

All is not lost, however. It was sometime before the scientific data on fluorocarbons was accepted as solid proof that the Earth's ozone layer was being depleted. And even after the information was irrefutable, special interests continued to resist the behavior modification demanded by this information feedback loop. Though the debate was often acrimonious, truth ultimately prevailed, and behaviors were modified. Most of us now accept that it is wrong to pollute the air with these chemicals.

I think that we would all agree that governments and differing administrations should behave ethically. However, it is equally clear that we do not always agree about what is ethical and what is not. Some may believe it is immoral to drill for oil in ANWR [Arctic National Wildlife Refuge], while others believe it is equally immoral not to drill. I have heard both arguments. The naturists who visit my office annually believe public nudity is, of course, natural, while others believe it to be immoral. Can biologically-based ethics resolve these differences in belief? I believe the answer is yes, eventually. Once, for example, there were those who believed it was wrong to put fluoride in water, but eventually the benefits were proven, time passed and most people changed their minds about there being any danger from fluoride.

Changing Morality

The change of mind about what is moral or immoral comes from either the understanding of new information or the application of information. This should give us hope. It is within our ability to adapt to new information that sustains the evolutionary process. Our minds are capable of reflecting upon our actions. So not only is information provided as raw data, but also it can be manipulated through contemplation and merged with existing information. In other words, it is a continual process of refinement, and this refinement is fundamental to evolution.

It is my firm belief that when we are in the midst of political conflict over an idea, proposal, new law, or a regulation—when we argue about whether or not we should drill in the Arctic or allow snow machines in parks; or when we dispute the veracity of some new information—we are, in fact, watching ourselves evolve. And we are evolving new codes of moral and ethical behavior that will ultimately contribute to the survival of the species. We as individuals may never see the end result, but the species as a whole may.

We are unique in that we are sentient beings with the capability of observing our own evolution. We now have a base of knowledge and understanding sufficient to modify our behavior even before we are confronted with the reality of the many threats that could destroy us. We have sown the seeds of our own destruction countless times and survived because we were able to modify our behavior in time.

But we are living in even more dangerous times now. The consequences of the use of certain information we receive are not always apparent. We rush headlong to gain advantage without recognizing the possible disadvantages. We have been lucky so far. We stop the car just before it goes over the precipice.

The Evolution of Ethics

The point is simply this: ethics also evolve, and this evolution of ethics flows naturally from our biological evolution. From the survival of a glob of genetic material to the survival of complex species, information feedback loops enhance survivability. Likewise, the ethics we develop are a result of the continuous acquisition of information and the corresponding response to that information. If we can better understand what E. O. Wilson calls, "the biology of moral sentiments," perhaps we can refine even further the evolution of our ethical systems and eliminate some of the conflict currently inherent in the meeting of science and politics.

Wilson believes we can understand the biology of moral sentiments and offers a prescription for doing so. We must, he says, define moral sentiments, first by precise descriptions from experimental psychology and then by analysis of the underlying neural and endocrine responses. We must also understand the genetics of moral sentiments, and this is most easily approached through measurements of the heritability of the psychological and physiological processes of ethical behavior and, eventually and with difficulty, through identification of the prescribing genes.

Understanding the development of moral sentiments as products of the interactions of genes and the environment is also important, according to Wilson. Research is most effective

Pope John Paul II on the Relationship Between Theology and Science

[Science] develops best when its concepts and conclusions are integrated into the broader human culture and its concerns for ultimate meaning and value. Scientists cannot, therefore, hold themselves entirely aloof from the sorts of issues dealt with by philosophers and theologians. By devoting to these issues something of the energy and care they give to their research in science, they can help others realize more fully the human potentialities of their discoveries. They can also come to appreciate for themselves that these discoveries cannot be a genuine substitute for knowledge of the truly ultimate. Science can purify religion from error and superstition; religion can purify science from idolatry and false absolutes. Each can draw the other into a wider world, a world in which both can flourish.

John Paul II, "Letter of Pope John Paul II to the Reverend George V. Coyne, S. J., Director of the Vatican Observatory," June 1, 1988, http://trimilenio.com

when conducted at two levels: the histories of ethical systems as part of the emergence of different cultures, and the cognitive development of individuals living in a variety of cultures. Such investigations are already well along in anthropology and psychology. In the future, they will be augmented by contributions from biology.

Wilson also encourages us to research and understand the deep history of moral sentiments to find out why they exist in the first place. Presumably, they contributed to survival and reproductive success during the long periods of prehistoric time in which they genetically evolved. He states:

From a convergence of these several approaches the true origin and meaning of ethical behavior may come into focus. If so, a more certain measure can then be taken of the strength and flexibility of the epigenetic rules composing the various moral sentiments. From that knowledge it should be possible to adapt ancient moral sentiments more wisely to the swiftly changing conditions of modern life into which, willy-nilly and largely in ignorance, we have plunged.

To say that what Wilson is describing is most difficult is an understatement. His statement should probably be qualified by saying, "if we don't kill ourselves first." This is not hyperbole when you realize that most scientists agree that nearly ninety-five percent of all species that ever existed are now extinct. Survivability is a risky business. Some would say, and I would agree, that survivability is our need for the third superordinate reference, namely abstract or transcendent concerns that enhance the quality of life. These transcendent concerns are embodied in religious beliefs, customs, and rituals. They are often the result of our natural instincts to wonder and question. A large part of the reason for my chosen profession is because the National Parks, indeed the natural world when seen through the eyes of a good interpretive ranger, provokes one to a sense of wonder and awe that leads to deep questions about why we exist, and how this wondrous thing called life can be at all. Our survivability is greatly enhanced by all this because it leads to the formation of what I call deep rules that guide our behavior towards one another; for example, love thy neighbor as thyself, the code of Hammurabi, the Ten Commandments, the precepts of Confucius and Socrates, or the code of non-violent resistance to injustice.

Think of the countless human beings that would have been slain during the struggles for civil rights, had it not been for this transcendent notion of non-violent resistance. Or think of the number of conflicts that might constantly arise if our churches did not admonish us to love our neighbors. Survival of our species is dependent on these transcendent concerns that lead us to form moral laws. Though some, most notably Steven J. Gould [in *Bully for Brontosaurus: Reflections in Natural History*], attempt to keep separate religion and science or morality and an objective, biologically based right and wrong, this attempt is misguided. In what can only be characterized as the mystical aspect of the mind's activity, namely faith, rules of morality have been developed in the apparent absence of any informational feedback loops. But the mind makes connections that we are not always aware of and produces thoughts in quiet contemplation that culminate in bursts of genius, often in the form of moral constructs. Just because we do not yet fully understand this more mystical side of our nature does not mean we should ignore it.

Taken together, our concern with our survival and our concern with the abstract or transcendent, serve as powerful motivators in the evolutionary process leading the species to what I believe will be a glorious never ending. Though public policy making is often contentious, contradictory, time consuming, and even farcical at times, so too has been the story of our evolution on this planet thus far. And so it will be until we do reach that glorious never ending.

> *"Ethics isn't ethics until other people are involved."*

Society Contributes to Ethical Behavior

Randy Cohen

An American humor writer, journalist, and philosopher, Randy Cohen writes the weekly "Ethicist" column in the New York Times Magazine. *In the following viewpoint, excerpted from his book* The Good, the Bad, and the Difference: How to Tell Right from Wrong in Everyday Situations, *Cohen argues that most people behave no better or worse than their neighbors. He contends that when making ethical decisions, individuals look to what others in their society tend to do in like situations and make similar choices. According to Cohen, individuals behave more ethically if the society in which they live is ethical.*

As you read, consider the following questions:

1. What flaw does Cohen find with the heroic model of ethics?
2. How does the author describe the relationship between etiquette, ethics, and politics?
3. How does Cohen relate ineptitude to evil?

T he mail sent to "The Ethicist" offers an impressive picture of people sincerely struggling to be good. But if these letters exist in the foreground, they imply a background of action without inquiry. For every question posed, there are many more that are never asked at all. It would, of course, be impossible to pause and question the propriety of each of our actions. Such constant analysis would be immobilizing, or at least so time consuming that we'd never get out of the house, stuck by the closet door as we pondered the acceptability of leather shoes. Rather than subject every decision of daily life to moral scrutiny, most of us act as our culture directs, behaving no better and no worse than our neighbors. In his profound and moving book, *The Face of Battle,* the British military historian John Keegan considers the question of why, when faced with the horror and suffering of combat most soldiers don't simply run away. He concludes that they are motivated not by high ideals of patriotism, not by ideology, not by anything one would identify as ethics. Keegan sees these soldiers standing fast so as not to be the least worthy among those assembled. And by that he does not mean the entire army, but those few men nearby. Keegan suggests that even under the most extreme and appalling conditions, most of us will behave about as well as our neighbors.

Something similar has been observed in the early careers of police officers. If a rookie cop is assigned to a corrupt station house, he stands a good chance of being corrupted himself. Put the same young officer in a clean station, and there's a very good chance he'll turn out to be an honest cop. His or her personal ethics hardly come into it.

In *Fast Food Nation,* his muckraking book on the fast food industry, Eric Schlosser makes a related observation. He reports that a high percentage of the robberies committed against McDonald's and similar joints are perpetrated by former employees. Schlosser attributes this to a reaction to low pay, poor working conditions, the lack of a chance to advance, and union busting. He sees these crimes not merely as the perfidy of a sociopath who works the deep fryer, but as a predictable response to a deplorable (i.e., unethical) work environment. Schlosser cites a study by Jerald Greenberg, professor of management at the University of Ohio, an expert on workplace crime, who reports that "when people are treated with dignity and respect, they're less likely to steal from their employer. 'It may be common sense,' Greenberg says, 'but it's obviously not common practice.' The same anger that causes most petty theft, the same desire to strike back at an employer perceived as unfair, can escalate to armed robbery."

The Social Context of Ethical Behavior

This is not to depreciate individual virtue, but we are unlikely to understand any behavior if it is seen only as a matter of individual moral choice detached from any social context. And we are unlikely to significantly increase honorable behavior if we rely only on individual rectitude. There is a kind of ecology of ethics. No matter how much you hector them, most Spartans will act like Spartans; most Athenians will act Athenian.

Just as individual ethics can only be understood in relation to the society within which it is practiced, it is also true that individual ethical behavior is far likelier to flourish within a just society. Indeed, it might be argued that to lead an ethical life one must work to build a just society. That is, if most of us will behave about as well as our neighbors, it is incumbent on us to create a decent neighborhood. Every community is dynamic—Sparta or [television's] *Late Night*. We not only live in it, but by our actions we create it. And as important, our community exists not only in the world but in our minds. It forms our values even as we shape its structures.

Sadly, the very idea of civic life is increasingly out of favor, superseded by the values of the marketplace, privatized. The idea of public life is generous, encouraging you to see yourself as living among other people, and to identify yourself as one of those others, with common purpose and problems. The marketplace is where interests clash: The buyer's low price is the seller's lost profit. Privatization is a world of antagonists at worst, of autonomous, isolated figures at best. But in an age where all of our lives are interconnected—in our economy, our infrastructure, even in our health—this notion of the lone cowboy is a fantasy.

Civic life is a public park, paid for by all of us, enjoyed by all of us. Its ethical necessities demand that we act in ways that make other people's happiness part of its use. Private life is a walled pool in your backyard. You need consider no one else, you need compassion for no one else: You can fill it with piranha if you like.

My Ethics

When I respond to readers' queries, I work from this premise: Ethics is the rational determination of right conduct, an attempt to answer the question "How should I act now?" Ethics is not just knowing; it is doing. And so it is necessarily a civic virtue, concerned with how we are to live in society; it demands an understanding of how our actions affect other people. There can be solitary sin—you can sit at home alone and covet your neighbor's ox—but there is no solitary unethical behavior. If you want to be unethical, you've got to get up, get dressed, get out of the house, and actually try to con your neighbor out of his ox. That is, ethics isn't ethics until other people are involved.

In considering an ethical question, whether concerning the right conduct of an individual or the society within which we function, I refer to a set of principles I cherish as profoundly moral. This constellation of values includes honesty, kindness, compassion, generosity, fairness. I embrace actions that will increase the supply of human happiness, that will not contribute to human suffering, that are concordant with an egalitarian society, that will augment individual freedom, particularly freedom of thought and expression.

It can be difficult to satisfy any one of these principles without neglecting another. To answer an ethical question placed before me, I must mediate among them as if they were quarreling factions, each with its own demands. This is an approach to ethics that requires something like diplomacy among the competing principles. My challenge is to devise a course of action that best serves all of these clamoring constituencies. Is there such a course? What behavior comes closest? It is ethics as problem solving.

Other People's Ethics

There are, of course, other ways to make ethical choices. One such method, transparency, advises us to act as if everyone in the community could see what we were doing. In a letter he wrote at Monticello on May 21, 1816, Thomas Jefferson recommended this to his young friend Francis Eppes:

> Never suffer a thought to be harbored in your mind which you would not avow openly. When tempted to do anything in secret ask yourself if you would do it in public. If you would not, be sure it is wrong.

This approach, tenaciously adhered to, would no doubt eradicate much bad behavior (and many naked aerobic workouts, if one were literal about the phrase "see what we were doing"). A limitation of this method is its essential conservatism. It does not encourage a rational system of decision making; it demands only that we live according to the conventions of our society. If you were a Hun and you indulged your taste for slaughter on horseback, Attila would love you, and your Hun buddies would admire you, but a thousand years later, you'd come in for a lot of criticism from many Americans. There is nothing in this approach that would stimulate reforms in Hun culture.

Ethical Culture

Felix Adler, the founder of the first Society for Ethical Culture and organizer of the American Ethical Union, believed that the nucleus of the spiritual life is to be found in the ethical relatedness of each person to others. It is because of our involvement in the lives of others that we are enabled to grow into moral and spiritual beings.

Adler expressed his insight in a deceptively simple maxim: "Act so as to encourage the best in others, and by so doing you will develop the best in yourself." This thought is what the term "ethical culture" was coined to suggest—the cultivation of ethical relationships on such a basis that the moral and spiritual potential of every member of the human community will be most fully activated. . . .

Our sense of right and wrong emerges out of the process of living together as social beings. . . .

Ethical Humanism is commitment to a way of life, to a creative relationship to others and thereby to ourselves, in which metaphysical and theological arguments are set aside. Whether or not God exists may be an interesting question. But the answer to that question—if answerable at all—should make no crucial difference in how we ought to live, how we ought to treat our fellow beings. My ethical obligations and potentialities—and yours—remain exactly the same, whether God exists or does not exist. Our shared task is to live decently, compassionately, and caringly in the world we inhabit.

Edward L. Ericson, "The Humanist Way: An Introduction to Ethical Humanist Religion," 2004. www.aev.org.

A system more amenable to reform is that of the heroic model. When in a quandary, ask yourself this: What would Lincoln do? The benefit of this strategy is that it makes possible the transformation of society. Lincoln was able to issue the Emancipation Proclamation. The unfortunate thing about this system is that Lincoln is never around when you need him. Lacking his profound moral understanding, it is difficult to know just what he'd say about your perplexing circumstances. And even if death were no barrier to some kind of phone call, Lincoln doesn't drive a stick, or trade stocks online, or for that matter, know how to use a telephone. Would he be able to apply his genius to your particular problem?

We see a vivid example of the heroic model—albeit a fictional one—in Atticus Finch, that magisterial figure of Harper Lee's *To Kill a Mocking Bird*. In the book, and even more so in the movie where Gregory Peck's very tone of voice radiates compassion and understanding, Atticus Finch is presented as a thoroughly admirable man. He is wise. He is good. He is kind. And if everyone acted like Atticus Finch, segregation would still be the law of the land. His ethical behavior is applied only to the most immediate personal exchanges, the narrowest social encounters. It provides him with no way to challenge the status quo. If an injustice is enshrined by custom, Finch accepts it. It is then called a way of life, and he treats it with the respect it requires to endure forever. Thus Finch might bravely represent the defendant at a trial steeped in racism, but he is unable to seek any real reform in the society that demanded this trial. We find in Atticus Finch the limitations of an ethics based on the heroic model, of transparency, and of an ethics divorced from politics.

Another ethical tool many people find helpful is the categorical imperative: Act as if everyone were to do as you do. It is, alas, not entirely reliable. If everyone followed your lead and went to the beach today, it would be pretty crowded. If everyone kissed your wife, you'd have to buy an enormous

45

supply of Chap Stick. And yet kissing your wife, even at the beach, does seem a benign activity.

Some people employ the test of utilitarianism: Seek the greatest good for the greatest number. However, even if hanging an innocent guy in town square each day would deter crime, and thus do enormous good for the entire community, that hanged man is likely to object. People can be so selfish.

Unsurprisingly, the system of moral thought referred to by most of my correspondents is that of the religion in which they were raised, Christianity or Judaism more often than not. For many of these folks, there can be no ethical thought divorced from religion; the two are nearly synonymous. And while I was raised in an observant household (suburban Reform Judaism) and am undoubtedly affected by the experience, my approach to these questions is, at least overtly, resolutely secular. . . .

Relationships and Obligations

Regardless of what system of ethics one employs, it will be severely tested by the behavior of actual human beings, who seldom behave as systematically as the code by which one strives to assess them. For one thing, our sense of ethical obligation is very much affected by relationship of the people involved. You have a different set of responsibilities to your children than you do to your boss or to a customer in your shop or to a stranger on the street. These obligations are often unspoken, and hence we may not all agree what they are, leading to confusion and conflict. Further, these relationships, and their attendant obligations, are often multiple and hence contradictory: They overlap or clash. Your boss is also, to some degree, your friend. The shopkeeper's daughter goes to school with your son. In many situations, it is hard to know whether to kiss or to kick.

It is not the ethicist but the novelist who most skillfully limns the complex and subtle relationships and the unspoken obligations that bind people together. The ethicist is obliged to provide a concise and direct answer to the questions put to him; one that applies a broadly applicable principle. This means employing the approach of the lawyer, invoking the proper general rule—a rule that could be applied to every similar case—and so necessarily advising: You shouldn't shoot the guy. It would, however, be more congenial to me to employ the methods of the novelist, seeking not for the general but the particular. To do this, the column would have to be much longer, not so much for my answers, but so the questioner could present a more richly detailed picture of his situation. If I knew more about the complicated people involved, their long and tangled history, the mitigating circumstances and painful emotional blows, the financial pressures the cousin was under, the medical problems of the aunt, the romantic betrayal of the brother-in-law, the hundred ameliorating circumstances and exacerbating conditions, maybe the most honorable advice I could give would be: Shoot the guy. But you can't do that in four hundred words. That's why we read novels. And have gun control laws.

And so, considering one particular relationship, should you not have the same ethical obligations to any child you see on the street that you have toward your own? You have no more right to treat a strange child unkindly, but clearly you feel a more tender attachment to the child you know. Not necessarily a bad thing. You do indeed have a particular responsibility to that child. While it is fitting—indeed, inevitable—that you would feel a profound affection and sense of obligation to your own child, one must also deal honorably with strangers. One must be wary of an ethics that is based not on what we do but to whom we do it.

Is Ethics Etiquette? Is Ethics Politics?

Some forms of etiquette can be seen as ethics practiced on the small scale—in the number of people involved, in what's at stake. Much that is dismissed as mere etiquette does indeed have a moral foundation. . . . One way to understand right conduct is to imagine it on a continuum—etiquette, ethics, politics. And indeed, sometimes the column has been criticized for conflating ethics and politics. But I maintain that the difference between the two is artificial, if indeed there is a significant difference at all.

Sometimes, as with etiquette and ethics, the distinction is a matter of scale. If one guy robs you, it's ethics, but when 435 people rob you, it's politics—or the House of Representatives is in session. But surely the deliberations of that body are subject to an ethical analysis.

Politics can be a necessary expression of ethics: Often the only way to achieve an individual ethical goal is through group endeavor, i.e., politics.

Some political questions are not essentially ethical but a matter of two competing interests each with a morally legitimate claim. For instance, there is that cowboy movie classic: Should the land be used by the cattle herders or the sheep herders? There is a kind of partisan politics that an ethicist should, of course, eschew, no matter his personal feelings about cows. However, it is also his job to point out that the land belongs to the Navajo, and both the cattle and sheep herders should get permission before any grazing takes place. That is where what some call politics is quite properly a subject for ethical scrutiny.

An ethics that eschewed such nominally political questions would not be ethics at all, but mere rule following. It would be the ethics of the slave dealer, advocating that one always be honest about a slave's health and always pay his bills promptly. But surely any ethics worth discussing must condemn the slave trade absolutely, not quibble about its business practices.

Ethics and Incompetence

Much of the world's misery can be traced not to a lack of virtue but to a lack of ability—not wickedness but ineptitude.

The transportation system that mires you in traffic for an hour while thousands of cars spew pollutants, the leaky pipe at the nuclear power plant, the witless sitcom are not the work of evil people but of maladroits. And this is a sad thing. To be a great villain requires intelligence and skill and clarity of vision, qualities in short supply. Shakespeare's Richard III was a man of magnificent towering wickedness; Captain Joseph Hazelwood, the skipper of the *Exxon Valdez*, was a doofus. Great evil is achieved by few, but bungling is accomplished by many. Fortunately, we live in a nation where one must not choose between these two qualities; indeed, we sometimes find both within a single person, often with a Washington address.

It is possible for ineptitude to become evil. When you realize that you are not likely to excel in a position of responsibility and seek it out of vanity, your fumbling is transmuted into iniquity. Incompetence is unethical when it involves the casual use of duct tape in a bypass operation because somebody sipped malt liquor and dozed through key lessons in medical school. Persisting as a foul-up heart surgeon is not merely inept; it is wicked. To fulfill certain obligations one must perform ably or step down.

There are other times when one must allow for innocent errors rather than pounce on them as an opportunity to make a few bucks. When you notice someone drop his wallet, you don't swipe the cash. When you get the wrong change, you inform the cashier. This is not just a matter of ethics but of civility. It would be exhausting to live in a world where one slipup meant death or replacing all your credit cards. Living an ethical life obliges us to tolerate imperfections in others (and to hope others will tolerate our own).

> *"Ethics—ethical reasoning, ethical choice, ethical conduct—requires that we seek the truth, the pinnacle of life, in order to have a proper basis—the only legitimate basis—for achieving justice."*

People Behave Ethically Because They Reason

Gregory D. Foster

In the following viewpoint Gregory D. Foster argues that ethical decisions require people to think critically. When individuals consider a proposed act, they attempt to identify who will be harmed or helped by the act, and whether or not the act is consistent with established values. In searching for the truth, individuals learn how to behave ethically, Foster asserts. A graduate of the U.S. Military Academy at West Point, New York, Foster is a civilian professor at the National Defense University in Washington, D.C.

As you read, consider the following questions:

1. According to Foster, what modes of inquiry characterize critical thinking?
2. Why is critical thinking crucial to ethics, as defined by Foster?

Gregory D. Foster, "Ethics: Time to Revisit the Basics," *The Humanist*, March 1, 2003. Copyright © 2003 by Gregory D. Foster. Reproduced by permission.

3. How does the author define the relationship between truth and justice?

For starters, what is ethics actually all about? Ethics is about right and wrong:

"No man is prejudiced in favor of a thing knowing it to be wrong. He is attached to it on the belief of its being right."

—*Thomas Paine, The Rights of Man*

"We do not call anything wrong, unless we mean to imply that a person ought to be punished in some way or other for doing it; if not by law, by the opinion of his fellow creatures; if not by opinion, by the reproaches of his own conscience. This seems the real turning point of the distinction between morality and simple expediency."

—*John Stuart Mill, Utilitarianism*

Good and Bad

Ethics is about good and bad, or good and evil.

"Things then are good or evil, only in reference to pleasure and pain. That we call good, which is apt to cause or increase pleasure, or diminish pain in us; or else to procure or preserve us the possession of any other good or absence of any evil. And, on the contrary, we name that evil which is apt to produce or increase any pain, or diminish any pleasure in us: or else to procure us any evil, or deprive us of any good."

—*John Locke, Concerning Human Understanding*

Moral philosophy is nothing else but the science of what is good and evil in the conversation and society of mankind. Good and evil are names that signify our appetites and aversions, which in different tempers, customs, and doctrines of men are different and diverse men differ not only in their judgment on the senses of what is pleasant and unpleasant to the taste, smell, hearing, touch, and sight; but also of what is conformable or disagreeable to reason in the actions of common life. . . . So long as a man is in the condition of mere nature, which is a condition of war, private appetite is the measure of good and evil: and consequently all men agree on this, that peace is good, and therefore also the way or means of peace, which ... are justice, gratitude, modesty, equity, mercy, and the rest of the laws of nature, are good; that is to say, moral virtues; and their contrary vices, evil.

—*Thomas Hobbes, Leviathan*

Virtue and Vice

Ethics is about virtue and vice.

It seems to me that virtue is something other and nobler than the inclinations toward goodness that are born in us. Souls naturally regulated and well-born follow the same path, and show the same countenance in their actions, as virtuous ones. But virtue means something greater and more active than letting oneself, by a happy disposition, be led gently and peacefully in the footsteps of reason. He who through a natural mildness and easygoingness should despise injuries received would do a very fine and praiseworthy thing; but he who, outraged and stung to the quick by an injury, should arm himself with the arms of reason against this furious appetite for vengeance, and after a great conflict should finally master it, would without doubt do much more. The former would do well, and the other virtuously; one action might be called goodness, the other virtue. For it seems that the name of virtue presupposes difficulty and contrast, and that it cannot be exercised without opposition.

—*Michel de Montaigne, Essays*

Vice, the opposite of virtue, shows us more clearly what virtue is. Justice becomes more obvious when we have injustice to compare it to. Many such things are proved by their contraries.

—*Quintilian, Institutio Oratoria*

Ethics is about benefit and harm.

A man can confer the greatest of benefits by a right use of [such things as strength, health, wealth, generalship] and inflict the greatest of injuries by using them wrongly.

—*Aristotle, Rhetoric*

The two essential ingredients in the sentiment of justice are the desire to punish a person who has done harm, and the knowledge or belief that there is some definite individual or individuals to whom harm has been done.

—*John Stuart Mill, Utilitarianism*

Ethics is about propriety and impropriety.

Socrates. And will not the temperate man do what is proper, both in relation to the gods and to men—for he would not be temperate if he did not? Certainly he will do what is proper. In his relation to other men he will do what is just; and in his relation to the gods he will do what is holy.

—*Plato, Gorgias*

Without an acquaintance with the rules of propriety, it is impossible for the character to be established.

—*Confucius, The Analects*

Principles, Character, and Examples

But ethics isn't simply about all these things—right and wrong, good and bad, virtue and vice, benefit and harm, propriety and impropriety. So too is it about principle—fixed, universal rules of right conduct that are contingent on neither time nor culture nor circumstance:

If habit is not a result of resolute and firm principles ever more and more purified, then, like any other mechanism of technically practical reason, it is neither armed for all eventualities nor adequately secured against changes that may be brought about by new allurements.

—*Immanuel Kant, Introduction to the Metaphysical Elements of Ethics*

So too is it about character—the traits, qualities, and established reputation that define who one is and what one stands for in the eyes of others.

Nothing can possibly be conceived in the world, or even out of it, which can be called good, without qualification, except a good will. Intelligence, wit, judgment, and the other talents of the mind, however they may be named, or courage, resolution, perseverance, as qualities of temperament, are undoubtedly good and desirable in many respects; but these gifts of nature may also become extremely bad and mischievous if the will which is to make use of them, and which, therefore, constitutes what is called character, is not good.

—*Immanuel Kant, Fundamental Principles of the Metaphysics of Morals*

So too is it about example—an established pattern of conduct worthy of emulation.

When thou wishest to delight thyself, think of the virtues of those who live with thee; for instance, the activity of one, and the modesty of another, and the liberality of a third, and some other good quality of a fourth. For nothing delights so much as the examples of the virtues, when they are exhibited in the morals of those who live with us and present themselves in abundance, as far as is possible. Wherefore we must keep them before us.

—*Marcus Aurelius, Meditations*

And so too is it about conscience—"the voice of the soul," "the pulse of reason," "that inner tribunal," "the muzzle of the will," "the compass of the unknown," "a thousand witnesses".

The moral sense follows, firstly, from the enduring and ever-present nature of the social instincts; secondly, from man's appreciation of the approbation and disapprobation of his fellows; and thirdly, from the high activity of his mental faculties, with past impressions extremely vivid; and in these latter respects he differs from the lower animals. Owing to this condition of mind, man cannot avoid looking both backwards and forwards, and comparing past impressions. Hence after some temporary desire or passion has mastered his social instincts, he reflects and compares the now weakened impression of such past impulses with the ever-present social instincts; and he then feels that sense of dissatisfaction which all unsatisfied instincts leave behind them, he therefore resolves to act differently for the future—and this is conscience.

—*Charles Darwin, Descent of Man*

What Ethics Involves

There is more to ethics, of course, than just knowing what it is about. As important to understanding its nature is what it involves. Is there something about the process of ethical reflection and choice that distinguishes it from other modes of thought? Some years ago Clarence Walton, former president of Catholic University, suggested the following: "Ethics involves critical analysis of human acts to determine their rightness or wrongness in terms of two major criteria: truth and justice."

Walton would have us understand, first, that ethics has virtually everything to do with the quality—even more than the content—of our thinking. How we think may not guarantee a right or best answer but it dramatically improves the prospects of finding one in sound, defensible fashion. As [Blaise] Pascal observed: "All our dignity consists . . . in thought. . . . Let us strive then to think well; that is the foundation of all morality."

To think well is to think critically. Critical thinking—the conscious use of reason—stands clearly apart from other ways of grasping truth or confronting choice: impulse, habit, faith, and intuition.

Impulse is nothing more than unreflective spontaneity— the sudden whim of a mind on cruise control or autopilot. Given the magnifying and accelerating effects of the media, impulsiveness is much more likely than deliberation in characterizing the response of today's policy practitioners to the manifold crises that define contemporary political affairs.

Habit is programmed repetition, the routinization of thought by which we remove presumably mundane matters to our subconscious so they can be dealt with more efficiently or conveniently without the attendant need to constantly revisit first principles. For example this is what we do when we standardize, generalize, or stereotype.

Faith

Faith, in the words of Walter Kaufman, "means intense, usually confident, belief that is not based on evidence sufficient to command assent from every reasonable person." Intensity of feeling and insufficiency of evidence are the operative features here. The dictionary might tell us that faith is belief—in an idea, a person, an institution—without need of certain proof. For the true believer, though, it isn't just the certainty of proof that is unnecessary; evidence itself is superfluous, especially evidence that contradicts an established belief system, worldview, or doctrine. This is what cognitive dissonance is all about—the prevalent human tendency to ignore or reject events or data that run counter to one's preconceptions or predispositions. Though faith and trust may go hand in hand, blind faith typifies a deadening of the intellect that may just as readily produce intolerance, disrespect, and distrust. The nineteenth-century Swiss philosopher Henri Frederic Amiel noted: "Action and faith enslave thought, both of them in order not to be troubled or inconvenienced by reflection, criticism and doubt."

Intuition is what we colloquially refer to as gut feeling or sixth sense—a way of speculative "knowing" based more on experience (lived or vicarious) than on reason, more on our overall sensory apparatus than on the workings of the mind. It is in this sense that a superficial impression of what appears to be—traits, behaviors, tendencies—so often gives birth to deep-seated pseudo-knowledge of what is. Intuition is neither entirely conscious nor entirely rational. In the words of George Santayana: "Intuition represents the free life of the mind, the poetry native to it . . .; but this is the subjective or ideal element in thought which we must discount if we are anxious to possess true knowledge."

What distinguishes these various forms of "unreason" from critical thinking is the systematic, investigative nature of the latter. "If you wish to strive for peace of soul and pleasure," said Heinrich Heine, "then believe; if you wish to be a devotee of truth, then enquire." Thinking critically is a disciplined pattern of thought or mode of inquiry that requires three things: first, questioning—assertions, opinions, and givens—rather than accepting them at face value; second, seeking and weighing evidence on all sides of an issue, not just evidence that affirms one's beliefs; and third, employing rigorous logic to reach defensible conclusions.

Critical Thought

The object of critical thinking is to achieve a measure of objectivity to counteract or diminish the subjective bias that experience and socialization bestow on us all. Why should this be necessary? Because when we are dealing with matters of ethical concern, the well-being of someone or something beyond ourselves is always at stake. In the extreme, the lives of others may literally depend on the choices we make or don't make—whether we are jurors in a court of law judging the guilt or innocence of an accused, or policymakers committing the blood and treasure of society to a foreign venture. The quality of our thinking, then, is a measure of the investment we are willing to make in an issue or situation. As [Benedict] Spinoza said, "If we live according to the guidance of reason, we shall desire for others the good which we seek for ourselves."

What is it, then, that we should think critically about? Human acts, suggests [Kendall] Walton—human rather than nonhuman—rather than thoughts. We focus on things human for two reasons. First, humans presumably possess abilities—predominantly intellectual—that other living species do not: the ability to make moral judgments, to deal with abstract concepts, to extrapolate from one set of circumstances to another, to exercise free will that surpasses conditioned response. "It is characteristic of man," said Aristotle, "that he alone has any sense of good and evil, of just and unjust, and the like."

Accordingly, a second reason we focus on humans is that we expect more of them than we do of other species. We don't expect the dog or cat, or even the dolphin or chimpanzee, to contemplate the propriety of its actions, to refrain from harming others, or to display empathy. We do expect such things from humans. But we also have grown to expect humanity's imperfections to outweigh its potential with disturbing frequency. Thus Mark Twain was moved to observe, with cynical accuracy: "The fact that man knows right from wrong proves his intellectual superiority to other creatures; but the fact that he can do wrong proves his moral inferiority to any creature that cannot."

We focus on human acts because acts have demonstrable effects on others. "The great end of life," said T.H. Huxley, "is not knowledge but action." To know is merely to possess the truth. To act is to do, to make something happen, to get something done. Thoughts, in and of themselves, have tangible effects only if they are translated into acts. This assumes that thoughts and actions are separable, that one can act without thinking or think without acting, that it is possible to harbor hatred or prejudice, understanding or good will, in one's heart (or mind or soul) without actually putting such feelings into effect. It isn't always clear, of course, what constitutes action, and therein lies much moral ambiguity. Is speech an act? If I say I am homosexual, call someone a disparaging name, or advocate the overthrow of government, am I acting? Should I be held responsible for such thoughts? By the same token, is inaction action? If I do nothing—like possessing (but not using) nuclear weapons, ignoring genocide, or declining to pay United Nations dues—am I actually doing something?

Examining Human Acts

Why do we critically analyze human acts? To determine their rightness or wrongness. There are any number of bases for making such determinations.

We might rely on some principle, precept, or rule: a law, executive order, or regulation, for example, that mandates or prohibits something (such as full financial disclosure or political assassination or the mishandling of classified information); or more abstract guidelines for behavior, such as the Golden Rule, the Ten Commandments, or an honor code that proscribes lying, cheating, and stealing.

We might be guided by the anticipated consequences or effects of our actions. Who benefits, and who is harmed? Who benefits most or what is the greatest benefit? Who is harmed least or what is the least harm? What consequences matter—physical ones only or also psychological and emotional ones? Temporally and spatially proximate ones only or also more distant ones?

We might concern ourselves with the intentions or motives behind one's acts. Does it matter why we do (or fail to do) something—or are results all that count? Do intentions outweigh effects or not? If I unintentionally inflict harm (or do good), should I be held culpable (or receive credit)?

We might focus on the rights of those involved in, affected by, or having a stake in our choices. Who deserves or doesn't deserve what—conditionally or unconditionally? Are there fundamental, natural rights that all persons deserve to enjoy merely by virtue of being human? Do rights reflect underlying

Objectivist Ethics

If I were to speak your kind of language, I would say that man's only moral commandment is: Thou shalt think. But a 'moral commandment' is a contradiction in terms. The moral is the chosen, not the forced; the understood, not the obeyed. The moral is the rational, and reason accepts no commandments.

My morality, the morality of reason, is contained in a single axiom: existence exists—and in a single choice: to live. The rest proceeds from these. To live, man must hold three things as the supreme and ruling values of his life: Reason—Purpose—Self-esteem. Reason, as his only tool of knowledge—Purpose, as his choice of the happiness which that tool must proceed to achieve—Self-esteem, as his inviolate certainty that his mind is competent to think and his person is worthy of happiness, which means: is worthy of living. These three values imply and require all of man's virtues, and all his virtues pertain to the relation of existence and consciousness: rationality, independence, integrity, honesty, justice, productiveness, pride.

Ayn Rand, Atlas Shrugged, *1957.*

needs that all humans recognizably have? Whose rights and which rights take precedence over others?

Conversely, we might emphasize obligations, the flip side of rights. Do those with a stake in our choices bear certain obligations toward others? Do the powerful or those in authority have special obligations, for example? Does the possession of rights impose attendant obligations?

Or we might be guided by values—traits, behaviors, or qualities to which we ascribe some worth or importance. The question in every case, of course, is which values—which normative values (or virtues)—should we seek, and which should we consider more important than others. Zeno, the Greek Stoic philosopher, spoke of wisdom, courage, justice, and temperance as primary virtues. Aristotle spoke more expansively of justice, courage, temperance, magnificence, magnanimity, liberality, gentleness, prudence, and wisdom, in that order. But there are yet other salutary values that seem no less worthy of attention: compassion, competence, decisiveness, empathy, honesty, integrity, loyalty, reliability, tolerance, and vision—to name but a few. The most nettlesome and difficult moral dilemmas we face often revolve around value conflicts in which two or more positive values are at stake in a given situation: duty versus friendship, for example, or honesty versus compassion, or loyalty to subordinates versus loyalty to superiors.

Truth and Justice

When we seek to determine the rightness or wrongness of something, we should do so with two major criteria in mind: truth and justice. Ralph Waldo Emerson made the monumentally insightful observation that "truth is the summit of being; justice is the application of it [truth] to affairs." The two go hand in hand. Ethics—ethical reasoning, ethical choice, ethical conduct—requires that we seek the truth, the pinnacle of life, in order to have a proper basis—the only legitimate basis—for achieving justice. Justice served is ethics realized.

Truth is what is—conditions, occurrences, statements whose existence and nature are there to be confirmed or verified by observation or reason. To possess truth is to have knowledge, the expected outcome of critical reasoning. If we possessed the truth, we would know what is ethical. But therein lies the rub. Truth is inherently elusive, and our ability to grasp it is tenuous at best, even illusory. Take any truth claim that passes for a statement of fact by those who believe it. To cite just one example: in the matter of whether women should be permitted to serve in combat, these are among the commonly asserted "truths" that drive discussion of the issue and ultimately determine whether justice is served or denied:

Women are incapable of performing in combat.

Women are less aggressive and less courageous than men. Combat requires aggressiveness and courage.

Women destroy unit cohesion.

The presence of women creates sexual tensions that otherwise wouldn't exist.

Women require more protection than men. Women bring out natural protective tendencies in men.

A woman's place is in the home.

A minimally qualified man is preferable to a better qualified woman.

A woman has less of an obligation to serve than a man does.

The American people deserve the best defense the military can provide them.

Such claims pass for self-evident truth among those who are already thus predisposed. But such so-called truths are rarely anything more conclusive and unequivocal than arguable propositions that cry out for supporting evidence.

There is an old saying: "A man with a watch knows what time it is; a man with two watches isn't so sure." This aphorism suggests a number of things about certainty and doubt, fact and opinion, objectivity and subjectivity, perception, bias, conviction, and socialization. Truth, like beauty, may lie as much in the eye of the beholder as in the thing observed; there may be multiple claimants, all more or less equal in standing, to the same truth; two or more parties can observe the same thing but see something completely different, or even that the same party can observe the same thing over time but see something different each time. Believing something intensely, even if that belief is shared by others, doesn't necessarily make it true in some objective sense.

Truth

Truth—perhaps precisely because it is so difficult to grasp or discern—is the essential precondition for justice. If justice is to be served, other than by accident, it must be predicated on the truth. Of course in any given situation there may be multiple truths that we would like to have—or that we knowingly or unknowingly need.

Let us say the question at hand is how to respond—justly and justifiably—to the September 11, 2001, terrorist attacks on the United States. We would like to have the truth of what actually happened (however seemingly self-evident). We would want to know the truth of who did it, how it happened, why it happened, what its effects have been, and what the effects of particular responses will be (for example, will punishment deter future such incidents and enhance U.S. credibility?).

Or take global warming. If we are to respond to it appropriately (in a timely, conclusive, affordable manner that doesn't create or exacerbate harm for those affected), we clearly want to know the truth of whether it actually exists; whether it is temporary or permanent, natural or human-made, recurrent or not, widespread or confined; and what its causes, effects, and implications are.

Justice is about receiving one's due or getting what one deserves—whether we are talking about one's standing or status, one's access to valuable resources, or one's treatment at the hands of others. This could mean obtaining a proper (fair) share of humanity's or society's goods (wealth, perquisites, esteem, and basic necessities), or receiving appropriate rewards or punishments for what one has or hasn't done (from bonuses or promotions to criminal conviction or military retaliation). Why would (or should) we care, for example, if 5 percent of the population controls 95 percent of society's wealth; if particular people are advantaged or disadvantaged because of their birth or personal-attributes rather than because of their accomplishments; if a third-time minor drug offender is sentenced to a long prison term or a confessed murderer is set free on a legal technicality; if civilian noncombatants are subjected to the violence and destruction of war? Because in every case these are matters of justice and injustice.

Trust: The Bottom Line

Together, truth and justice constitute the basis for trust. Therein lies their ultimate importance in distinguishing what is ethical from what is not. As Sissela Bok observed in her thoughtful and perceptive 1978 book *Lying*: "Trust is a social good to be protected just as much as the air we breathe or the water we drink. When it is damaged, the community as a whole suffers; and when it is destroyed, societies falter and collapse. . . . Trust and integrity are precious resources, easily squandered, hard to regain."

Trust is social glue. It is what unites rather than divides, what turns a gaggle of individuals into a community with a sense of oneness. If I am sure I can count on you to tell me the truth, to seek the truth where I am concerned, to treat me fairly, to care whether I get what I deserve and deserve what I get, then our relationship is more likely than not to be defined by trust. Where such trust exists—thinking, not blind, trust; lasting, not momentary, trust—the prevalence of ethical conflict and the burden of ethical choice are materially diminished. Restoring trust thus is the great task of ethics, and understanding ethics accordingly is the great task before humanity today.

"The interest in character education is very much from parents and schools ... asking, 'How can we better influence the kind of people that our kids become?'"

Schools Can Teach Children to Behave Ethically

Steve Johnson, interviewed by Kirk O. Hanson

In the following interview, conducted by Kirk O. Hanson, the executive director of the Markkula Center for Applied Ethics in Santa Clara, California, Steve Johnson maintains that many children now learn how to behave ethically at America's schools since their parents no longer make the time to teach them ethics. According to Johnson, character education programs can help teach students about respect, responsibility, integrity, and other positive virtues. As director of character education at the Markkula Center, Johnson developed the character-based literacy curriculum used in California community schools.

As you read, consider the following questions:

1. What is the triangle model of moral development, as argued by Johnson?

2. What are the eight key values that Johnson's character education program promotes?

Kirk O. Hanson and Steve Johnson, "Teaching Values in School: An Interview with Steve Johnson, S.M.," *Issues in Ethics*, vol. 13, Summer 2002. Copyright © 2005 by the Markkula Center for Applied Ethics. Reproduced by permission.

3. According to Johnson, what factors in parent-child inter-actions have changed the way kids are socialized in modern society?

K irk O. Hanson: *Steve, let me begin with a simple question: What is character education?*

Steve Johnson: Schools have always been interested in three kinds of outcomes:

1. skills—what our students are able to do

2. knowledge—what they know

3. character—the kind of people they become

Sometimes character is talked about in terms of citizen-ship. When I was in school, we used the term *deportment*. But whatever we call it, as educators, we've always been interested in building positive, productive citizens.

What are the objectives of character education in the schools today?

In some schools, it's about promoting pro-social thoughts, values, and behaviors and having students act as good citizens should in school. In others, it's about developing specific de-sirable values. For schools in general, character education is about finding some way to help students develop good habits or virtues.

What is your approach to character education and how does it differ from other approaches?

We say that character education is a way of doing every-thing in the school. It's not one particular program or focus; it's everything we do that influences the kind of human beings students become.

The Triangle Model

To break that down, we use a triangle model to explain moral development. Basically, we look at three sets of factors that in-fluence how human character develops.

The left section of the triangle deals with values. We recognize that there are core common values, and we are socialized to develop them through:

1. role models, such as parents, other adults, peers, and mass media
2. legends and heroes, people we look up to
3. stories and narratives in print, film, TV, or video games
4. reinforcement (We're all more likely to continue to do what pays off or works for us.)

At the same time, coming from the right side of the triangle, are thought processes. These are the rational, cognitive ways we grapple with the moral life, and they include:

1. problem solving processes for helping to make choices
2. thinking in a way that is clear and straight, not distorted; seeing many possibilities in a situation—shades of gray instead of black and white
3. the ability to reflect on our experience and to learn from it
4. the ability to use a framework to make decisions when we genuinely don't know what to do in a hard case

The triangle sits on the foundation of skills, which we group into two sets: coping and cooperation. To understand coping skills, think about the moments in our lives when we have the most trouble and ask, What else was going on at the same time? Were we tired or stressed or angry? In order to build character, we have to learn to deal with the times when it's hard to be the kind of person we want to be. Those coping skills are emotional management, anger control, impulse control, stress management, and so forth. Cooperation skills include dealing with people and dealing with conflict situations.

In every lesson we do, in every program we put on, we balance the triangle, taking into account values formation,

Character Education

The development of a culture of character is crucial to the well-being of our nation.

For this great nation to sustain its prominence, we must do a better job educating our children. But we must teach them more than reading and math, we must also teach them the values upon which this nation was built. . . .

We face formidable forces: music, movies, the arts, and culture itself teach our students to prize greed, celebrity, indifference, disregard, and violence.

In some schools, gangsta rap and criminal deeds are tolerated, even allowed to replace education itself. We have to teach tolerance. But we do not have to tolerate the absence of positive values.

We have to remind our students of a lesson taught in Ancient Greece: the character of the person is the primary product of education. Good character is the product of good judgments made every day. Good character is a reflection of someone with good judgment, seeking wisdom, acting virtuously. Good character becomes the second nature of the person who values truth, wisdom, hard work, compassion, empathy, and enlightenment. In Plato's time, the word "character" meant something like "the mark, the stamp or the impression on the person." When the educational system works well, the best indicator is the character of its students. We see the indelible mark of the school upon the student.

Rod Paige, "Remarks of Secretary Paige at the Character Education Partnership 10th Anniversary Dinner," October 16, 2003. www.ed.gov.

thought processes, and skill development. That's our reference point.

Another thing that makes our program distinct is that we said right from the beginning, "We are not going to be another character education program that's just for the most privileged. If it doesn't work for kids who read across the spectrum—below the 20th percentile as well as above—and if it doesn't work for kids who have trouble in school as well as those who don't, and if it doesn't work for kids who like school and kids who hate school, it isn't for real."

Why do you work with the language arts curriculum?

We wanted to tie the program to things schools already need to do. We spend so much time on the English language arts program because everyone takes English, and the curriculum is already full of strong narratives that provide an excellent vehicle for character education. Literacy is fundamental.

Universal Values

Do you have to teach character education to kids in the mainstream differently from the way you teach at-risk youngsters?

I don't think so. Kids throughout the population face the same needs, the same challenges, the same realities in their lives. Perhaps more privileged youngsters have been able to struggle with them better because they've had more nurturing, better role models, wider opportunities, and so forth. But the substance is very much the same.

What about differences in culture and language?

Ethics is not about being part of any culture; it's about being human. Whatever your background, culture, language, etc., you cannot be successful, you cannot run a society without human minimums in the way of conduct.

When I work with groups, I take the core values and I go around and ask if anyone is opposed to them: "Is anyone around here opposed to respect, at least in the way other people treat you? Is anyone opposed to responsibility, at least in the way someone drives if he borrows your car? Is anyone here opposed to self-control, at least by the person holding a gun in the same room with you?" And so forth. What we find is everyone realizes right away that these are human minimums.

Even the most jaded kids recognize the importance of values. Now, they may not be able to demonstrate them, but they at least agree that values are significant. For example, no matter how disrespectful they are toward other people, kids are very clear that they would like people to respect them.

Where did you get the specific values that are taught in your program and why those?

That took a long, long time. When we look at values and virtues, there's no end to the list. Actually, we came to ours from a couple of different directions. One was Thomas Lickona's work on educating for character. His notion is that two virtues, respect and responsibility, frame a public, teachable morality.

Respect is the regard due to me and to all other persons on the planet by virtue of our being human. It's not honor or something we have to earn, but precisely that which we don't. Respect forms the restraint side of morality. It's what I restrain myself from doing because it might harm that which I value.

Responsibility is the positive, proactive side of morality— the things I do because I said I would, because I ought to, because they promote the common good.

We see respect and responsibility as the two hinges of a public, teachable morality, which integrity fills in. When we say "integrity," we mean the whole person, undivided, developing all aspects of the self.

But you go beyond respect, responsibility, and integrity.

Reaching All Children

Yes. We were interested in what happens to young people who score below the 20th percentile on standardized tests and who may have a history of anti-social behavior. We wondered what virtues we could emphasize that might make a difference in the thoughts, values, and behaviors of those kids. What helps people to be more pro-social than anti-social, more virtuous than criminal? What could keep someone who's having trouble from continuing to get in more trouble?

So we looked at research not only in the usual places— such as philosophy—but also in special education, correctional education, and criminology. We looked at psychological research on cognitive distortions that cause people to twist their filter of reality in a way that causes them to mis-see and mis-think about the world. And we looked at virtues that were a counter to the misperceptions that get people in trouble. In that process, we realized that virtues like self-direction and self-control are important.

We also saw that many at-risk kids valued courage, but they had a self-destructive vision of it. To them, the most courageous thing you could do was the most outrageous thing you could do. The more dangerous it was, the more courageous they thought it was. We try to teach the idea that courage is about risk, but for a purpose not for a thrill. Courage is about risk that promotes some greater good, which justifies the danger. So courage gets linked to the idea of self-control. We also developed a unit called "change requires effort," in which we teach that change is both desirable and requires work in the way we go about it.

In addition, we're interested in values like moderation because we work with many kids who tend to go to one extreme or the other, for example relative to drinking or using drugs. In this area, we try to help them find a way to moderate their impulses and desires.

And we focus on justice, which for us means recognizing that there are other people in the world and that they make legitimate demands on us. When we work with kids, we always start by saying, "Ethics might not be necessary if you were the only one here, but you're not. Because we have to share this planet with other people, we have to have some way of getting along together. We call that ethics. Ethics is about relationships, and justice is necessary in order to preserve those relationships."

So, respect, responsibility, integrity, self-control, self-direction, change requires effort, moderation, and justice—those are the eight key values that frame our program.

Tell us about a core value unit. How do you teach self-control?

Typically a unit is two months long and involves a variety of activities arranged under four levels:

1. Which of the California Language Arts Standards does the unit address?

2. What texts will we use?

3. What products will students create?

4. What processes will we use to teach the big ideas in the unit?

We start with a basic understanding of the value. With self-control, we use the notion of courage and risk for a purpose and the idea that courage requires self-control. You've got to be able to manage yourself in order to take purposeful risks.

The Importance of Classic Literature

To Kill a Mockingbird is the core work in this particular unit. In addition to our core novel, we have several hundred other items that teachers might choose from, including novels, poetry, nonfiction, plays—all of them dealing with the courage theme.

Of course, the unit is embedded in the English language arts curriculum, and, as it happens, the standards that are addressed in this particular unit involve academic proficiencies such as writing narrative responses to literature and exposition. Actually, the unit cuts across the six language arts: reading, writing, listening, speaking, feeling, and visually representing.

With each text, we work with students to create a visual product, which they then explain and eventually turn into written language. In a classroom that's studying *To Kill a Mockingbird* right now, students started by making a bookmark that represented the town. As they made that bookmark, they indicated where all the various places in the town were, which not only helped them to keep track of where they were in the story but also gave them a visual reference point as we talked about the place.

In the first four weeks, we did open-mind portraits, for which students created a bust of a key character in the story. Then they surrounded that character with cartoon bubbles, which included things that character might think or say. As the unit goes on, they'll add bubbles in different colors to show how they see that character changing through the story, and they'll make open-mind portraits of other characters, as well.

They may also make posters. One of the things kids notice right away is the subject of racism in *To Kill a Mockingbird*. To address that issue directly, we have them make posters with some solutions they might suggest for dealing with that problem. When we get to the courtroom scenes, we do an actual cross-examination and create a newspaper to show what happens.

We follow each of these activities with daily journal writing, where the kids are really looking at characters and how they exhibit courage. Eventually, we ask them to choose the character they think is most courageous and, in small groups, they create a campaign ad for that particular character. We also have them do negative ads about characters that they think don't exemplify courage, and why not.

After we put those ads up, we ask them to do a radio show, which they then write a paragraph about. The following week, we teach them how to turn that paragraph into an essay, where they compare four characters as to courage, with an introduction and conclusion about how their definitions of courage have changed.

Room for Variety

Every teacher who works on this unit is going to do it somewhat differently. We offer about 100 basic strategies that we mix and match in various ways, but all of them include visual and oral language products that eventually turn into written language processes. Throughout, we're really looking for ways that move the kids to think about values. We test and try to change kids' concept of courage so that it includes a willingness to use skills such as anger control and anticipating the consequences of actions.

Your program is now operating in more than 200 schools. In fact, character education has been a very popular idea nationally during the past 10 to 15 years. Why is it on the public agenda so prominently?

I think a lot of people are afraid of the kind of society we're becoming. Oftentimes, they think there's some significant difference between kids today and kids "like we were," and they believe things are deteriorating.

I'm not sure things are deteriorating, but we're all often startled by the world we see. Some people find it easy to blame the schools and say, "The problem is based on character defects, and the schools should teach character." Others say it's about parents and the need for them to take their jobs more seriously.

I think we've almost lost interest in raising children in this society, and a good deal of our problem comes from that. Kids today spend more time with their peers and less time with adults than has ever been true in history. The result is that kids socialize one another.

If we want to have more impact on our children's values, we have to be willing to devote more time to them. I remember the myth of the one-minute manager and that somehow you could apply this to parenting. But it's not about quality time; it's about time.

The interest in character education is very much from parents and schools feeling that they're not doing a good enough job and asking, "How can we better influence the kind of people that our kids become?"

Periodical Bibliography

The following articles have been selected to supplement the diverse views presented in this chapter.

Mike Fleischmann	"What Did Jesus Do? The Seven Priorities That Guided Jesus' Decisions Can Help Us in Our Daily Choices," *Christian Reader*, September/October 2003.
Bobby Fong	"Of Character and Citizenship," *Peer Review*, Summer 2002.
Keith Green	"The Evolution of Morality and Religion: A Biological Perspective," *Religious Studies*, September 2005.
Joshua D. Greene et al.	"An MRI Investigation of Emotional Engagement in Moral Judgment," *Science*, September 14, 2001.
Dan Johnson	"A Shift in Moral Authority," *Futurist*, November 2001.
T.J. Mawson	"God's Creation of Morality," *Religious Studies*, March 1, 2002.
Richard B. Miller	"On Making a Cultural Turn in Religious Ethics," *Journal of Religious Ethics*, September 2005.
Robert F. Morse	"Humanism: One Activist's View," *Free Inquiry*, Fall 2001.
Wolfhart Pannenberg	"When Everything Is Permitted," *First Things: A Monthly Journal of Religion and Public Life*, February 1998.
William Rusher	"What Can God's Ten Rules Do?" *Conservative Chronicle*, September 8, 1999.
Kevin Ryan and Karen Bohlin	"Teacher Education's Empty Suit," *Education Week*, March 8, 2000. www.edweek.org.

CHAPTER 2

Why Should People Behave Ethically?

Chapter Preface

People act ethically because they recognize an obliging force or circumstance that demands ethical behavior. These forces or circumstances range from a supernatural creator who demands moral behavior to a feeling of obligation to future generations. For example, the belief that God desires people to live ethical lives is enough to establish in some people a comprehensive moral approach to life. These people believe that they should behave ethically in order to please God. For others, the needs of future generations provide strong motivation for ethical behavior. These thinkers believe that people should behave ethically so that their children will inherit a better world.

Reasons to behave ethically are not always so abstract, however. People often behave ethically in order to reap some immediate benefit or avoid a negative consequence. For example, business owners may establish company codes of ethics that outline standards of behavior for their employees. They know that doing so will help them stay clear of legal troubles. By avoiding corporate malfeasance, they can ensure that their customers and investors remain confident in them, which is obviously good for business. They also guarantee that they avoid having to pay legal fees associated with lawsuits. Thus, by formulating a code of ethics, companies aim to maximize positive consequences and minimize negative ones.

The same dynamics can be seen in politics. Politicians know that if they behave ethically, their constituents are more likely to continue voting for them. Conversely, if they are caught acting unethically, their constituents likely will not vote for them again. If caught in political wrongdoing, they might even be indicted by a grand jury, which could spell high legal costs and an end to their political careers. Thus, a politician considering voting for a certain bill in order to "pay back" a campaign contributor who will benefit from the passage of the legislation has to consider what will happen should such a link become known. At risk is his or her political career and financial stability.

On a personal level people often behave ethically so that they can gain the respect of their family, friends, and employers. Being well thought of feels good and can net certain benefits, such as invitations to enjoyable social events or promotions at work. Individuals also behave ethically to avoid problems, such as being fired for stealing from the workplace or being sued for divorce after having an affair. Individuals wondering how to act in any given situation must weigh both the benefits and costs of certain actions before proceeding.

To be sure, many people behave ethically to serve what they feel are higher obligations to God and society, but people also act morally in order to benefit themselves and avoid negative consequences. In the following chapter authors consider the many reasons, both high-minded and practical, for behaving ethically.

> *"In the present crisis of our planet the greatest virtue or moral imperative is the care and rejuvenation of Earth and securing the right of all people to its natural bounty."*

People Should Behave Ethically to Preserve the Environment

John McConnell

John McConnell is the founder of International Earth Day and a lifelong advocate for peace, international cooperation, and the environment. In the following viewpoint, which the author presents as a set of theses on the care of the earth, McConnell argues that people have an ethical responsibility to protect the earth. The environment, upon which all people depend, is being destroyed, he asserts. In order to protect the well-being of all the world's people, a unified movement to protect the earth must be started, McConnell maintains.

As you read, consider the following questions:

1. According to McConnell, what benefits to humanity will be derived from the campaign for the care of the earth?

2. In the author's opinion, what role does religion play in humanity's understanding of its rights to use the earth?

3. What determines the value of religious faith or philosophical belief, according to McConnell?

Earth Danger

1. RECOGNIZING: That ignorance and neglect of our planet, combined with the folly of international rivalries, has now endangered all life on Earth;

2. That our planet's life is threatened by policies and actions that cause massive pollution of air, water and soil and dangers of chemical, biological and nuclear disaster;

3. That mutual trust is necessary in order to counter these threats;

Mutual Trust

4. That only by open communication and joint action, for a great common good, can mutual trust develop;

5. That the one thing we have in common is our planet;

Campaign for Earth

6. That a campaign for the care of Earth will create relationships leading to mutual trust and ultimately to reciprocal disarmament and stable peace;

7. That in pursuing peace it is important to identify and emphasize vital matters and the extent and nature of our accord, and to build on this accord;

8. That peaceful actions beget peace;

9. That in a world of instant global communications a strong, informed public opinion in all nations dedicated to peace and care of Earth, could become the greatest deterrent to war and to local violence;

10. That the greatest challenge in history is the present challenge of destiny involving all humanity; a challenge to reclaim the Earth for all peoples and to free them from the fear of war and want;

11. That accepting this challenge will bring the measure of trust needed to achieve these goals;

Wholehearted Dedication Needed

12. That the peaceful care of our planet cannot be accomplished through half-hearted or insincere efforts, but will require the dedication of all humanity;

13. That in seeking the basic change in the conduct of governments and their peoples, we acknowledge the failures of all previous efforts to achieve a peaceful world;

14. That investments worldwide in instruments of destruction endanger the human race;

15. That excessive destruction of trees, vegetation, and wildlife, from ancient times to the present, has decimated or destroyed numerous species and degraded Earth's potential for nurturing life, and that the current acceleration of this process will bring global catastrophe if it is not soon brought to a halt;

Humanity's Space Age Choice

16. That world peace requires a basic long-term commitment to change attitudes and conduct, and to develop structures and programs that will foster peaceful progress in the care of Earth and in our relationships with each other;

17. That new factors in the quest for peace are Space Age global awareness and deep concern everywhere that something must be done;

18. That we owe to untold generations in our past and future a firm decision for peace and care of Earth;

19. That it is time for humanity to take charge and take care of their planet;

Nurture of Earth

20. That the campaign for Earth requires ideas and attitudes conducive to the nurture and care of Earth;

21. That loyalty to community, bioregion, and planet is essential for the healing of our planet and people;

22. That a patriotism embracing people and planet as well as nations is necessary now;

23. That loyalty to our planet will not hurt, but instead will help our lesser loyalties;

Allegiance to Earth

24. That while national governments use police force to coerce allegiance when needed, their long-term strength depends on voluntary support by their citizens;

25. That loyalty to our planet can best be achieved through voluntary efforts to understand its life systems and processes, and then with love for our planet to help nurture and sustain the amazing web of life that covers our globe;

26. That global communication and education to foster Earth's care can provide the measure of enlightenment needed to justify and assert the authority of humanity in the management and care of Earth;

Global Community of Conscience

27. That voluntary support of Earth care and person-to-person communication about Earth care can provide a global communication of conscience dedicated to Earth's protection. This will bring inner peace and global peace;

28. That constraints and requirements for Earth care will then permeate society and provide our global conscience with moral authority and influence greater than that of national governments;

29. That as we develop a strong community commitment of individuals and governments to the care of Earth and to one another, and are aided by world public opinion filled with hope instead of fear, we will establish peaceful relationships and make any war unthinkable and impossible;

30. That the management and care of Earth by the people of Earth can only be achieved by their willing support;

31. That the willing support of people throughout our world can only be obtained by providing equitable, fair benefits in return for their services;

32. That it is necessary to determine the rights and responsibility of individuals in the care of Earth;

Rights to the Use of Earth

33. That religions teach, and philosophers aver that the Earth is for all people. The Psalms state, "The Earth hath He given to the children of men";

34. That, whether considered the gift of God, or the bounty of Nature, every individual has an equal claim, or right to Earth's natural bounty; to a portion or benefit from their share of Earth's land, raw materials and natural resources;

35. That every country should provide a free homestead for each family that lacks one, or the means to obtain one. Every person who wishes to receive this basic inheritance in their planet should be given a secure habitable shelter, or be provided the purchasing capacity or land and materials;

Fair Benefits from Earth

36. That expenses of government and public needs they serve can best be met by land use fees, or single tax, based on the value of the land (not on improvements or labor);

37. That every individual, regardless of circumstances or lack of resources, should be assured an opportunity for basic nutritious food, or practical means for procuring it;

38. That raw materials—oil, coal, minerals—are the inheritance of all Earth's people. As they are mined, sold, or used, at least 2 percent of their value should be equally distributed as royalties to everyone. These unearned assets in the ground, the inheritance of all Earth's people, should be carefully mined, conserved and recycled by the owners or managers, and used by consumers in ways that will increase the Earth's natural bounty and benefit Earth's people;

Responsibility for the Care of Earth

39. That rights to the bounty of Earth must be equaled by responsibility for its care;

40. That every individual should be taught from childhood the requirements for Earth care by instruction and experience in caring for gardens, animals, and birds. Later instruction should include Earth Care criteria and guidelines for land use, manufacturing, recycling, energy, design of homes and communities with sustainable goals in population and development; preservation of wildlife and wilderness areas, ways to diminish pollution of air, soil and water;

Money and Trade

41. That equitable trade and development requires a fair, honest medium of exchange;

42. That money should not be a product, controlled by special interests and sold to the highest bidder, but instead should be a free medium of exchange, based on things to be exchanged, and made available through collateral loans in percentages needed to facilitate trade and exchange without inflation;

43. That amply secured loans should not require payment of interest, only the cost of paper work. Usury (interest) is condemned by major religions. It can cause inflation and results in unearned and unnecessary income by manipulators;

44. That in high risk loans to individuals or firms, security provided by the borrower should be of equal value to money provided by the bank. And both should share equally in any losses or profits; in this case money is actually an investment instead of a loan;

Producers and Consumers

45. That control of capital should be widely dispersed and prevented from being used to take unfair advantages of indi-

viduals or corporations with legitimate need for money;

46. That public disclosure should be required in the management of any business or the sale of any stock setting forth the company's adherence to Earth Care criteria: Such as what is being done to avoid pollution in production and use of products or services; energy efficiency; design for easy repair, service and recycling of products; fair wages and benefits to employees. Reports of standards adopted and adherence should be provided by appropriate independent authorities;

47. That leaders in church, state and entertainment should urge support of Earth Trustee efforts and provide examples of an Earth Trustee conscience in investments, purchases and life style;

48. That individuals who invest for greatest profit with no regard for how the money is made—bombs for poor misguided countries, production lacking environmental safeguards, unfair poverty wages for employees—should be made aware of the harm they are causing. Companies responsible for such Earth Kill practices should be exposed, penalized and their products shunned until they convert to Earth Trustee conduct;

49. That the media should be the guardian of the public's long-term interest and could serve this purpose by exposing gross Earth Kill examples, and by headlining Earth Trustee solutions and programs;

Greed and What to Do About It

50. That a major cause of injustice, of crimes against Nature and people, is the way we have accepted and institutionalized greed, particularly greed for private profit from the land and natural resources of the Earth;

51. That most successes in selling products are presently achieved by advertising and promotion that increases greed, lust and vanity. Subtle motivational techniques are used to de-

Kirk. © 1992 by Kirk Anderson. Reproduced by permission.

ceive and corrupt and thereby make greater profits: For example, in the promotion and sale of cigarettes;

52. That to attain a viable Earth Trustee future it is essential that designers, inventors, planners, producers, and consumers—and advertising executives, all learn the necessity of Earth Trustee constraints. A massive educational program in schools, churches and voluntary agencies is needed to expose Earth Kill kinds of promotion and products and instead promote public awareness of Earth Trustee values and choices;

Education

53. That an Earth Trustee curriculum in schools is urgently needed. Earth Trustee studies can provide the best unifying purpose for education;

54. That it is essential for children to learn more about the wonders of Earth and that our generation can become trustees, custodians and caretakers of our beautiful planet;

55. That to accomplish these goals effective use must be made of every means of communication—print, fax, radio, TV, telephone, satellite, computer networks;

Media

56. That the general knowledge about how the world works should be constantly presented by media—in news and special programs. For example, the role of light, soil, water, air and living organisms in nurturing the thin skin of life that covers our globe; the diversity of plants, trees, animals, birds, insects—all necessary to the delicate balance of life-giving nutrients on our planet;

Technology

57. That technology must be used to foster Earth's care. The present mindless use of technology in ways that poison, pollute and disrupt Nature's ecosystems must be halted. Instead of a destroyer, technology can and must become a harmonious extender of Nature's bounty;

Right Size for Everything

58. That there is a right and wrong size for everything. Finding the right size is essential to the lasting success of any product, system, arrangement, institution or endeavor;

59. That everything should be as small as possible, unless there is a good reason for it to be larger. In many cases communities and businesses should be smaller—providing more intimate, humane services to smaller groups of people;

60. That constant growth of a city or a business will eventually lead to disaster. Exponential factors decree this. Cities and towns can avoid this by providing laws that only allow new construction which replaces old structures. New Earth communities using interactive technologies can relieve congestion;

61. That once a community or business reaches an optimum size, progress should be sought, not through an increase

in size or profits, but through improved quality of services and products. In a small business where the employees are close to owners with a personal interest in each employee, a shared understanding of the operation and its purpose brings better give and take, the pursuit of excellence and efficiency. Given a level playing field of competition, when a business gets too big, its smaller competitors will be the ones to increase sales. Also, cooperatives will be given a better chance to prove their worth;

Ethics of Religion

62. That a sense of responsibility and the practice of Earth Trustee ethics is an essential requirement for the future;

63. That major religions, philosophies and ideologies teach the "Golden Rule"—to do unto others as you would have them do unto you;

64. That while some people of faith are engaged in works of peace and works of charity, many religious people show in their actions bigotry and hypocrisy;

65. That the majority of people fail miserably to live up to their intentions;

66. That moral responsibility and ethical behavior is for the most part found in people of deep, religious faith—reflected in their compassion, fairness and charity;

67. That most conflicts over religious and ideological beliefs have their roots in different hypotheses about the unknown. Does God exist? What is the nature or purpose of reality?;

Key to Basic Accord

68. That in the question of what life is all about, we face profound mysteries and unanswerable questions. Who can imagine the Universe never having a beginning or ever having an end?;

69. That there is in the human spirit a desire for meaning in life. Religious belief, especially belief in a loving God, provides a more promising hypothesis about the unknown. While belief in God or life after death cannot be scientifically proven, there are phenomena that suggest its possibility; for example, answers to prayer, and reports by people who were briefly dead;

70. That the value and test in the here and now of religious faith or philosophical belief is its good effect on the believer: the measure of confidence, virtue, integrity and the practice of the Golden Rule;

Virtue

71. That in the present crisis of our planet the greatest virtue or moral imperative is the care and rejuvenation of Earth and securing the right of all people to its natural bounty;

A New Golden Age

72. That every adherent of ethics or religious faith should act as a responsible Trustee of Planet Earth: join the global Earth Trustee Effort and assist some Earth Care project;

73. That every municipality or community should form an independent Earth Trustee Committee, which will discuss the 77 Theses and then form their own program to help the Earth Campaign: initiating or assisting projects that eliminate poverty and pollution and benefit humanity;

74. That radio stations and TV need to program one or more daily Earth Minutes [at specified times throughout the day]. These simultaneous global "minutes without words" can be produced independently by any radio or TV station, with views and sounds of nature, children, music, bells, our planet;

75. That to foster the vital unity needed in our diversity, all individuals and institutions will celebrate Earth Day each year on the March Equinox—Nature's Day, March 20 or 21; the first day of Spring (Fall in the Southern Hemisphere);

76. That global acceptance of responsibility for the protection and care of Earth can usher in a new golden age of opportunity for all humanity;

77. THEREFORE, LET US PLEDGE OUR LIVES AND FORTUNES TO AID THE GREAT TASK OF EARTH'S REJUVENATION, AND WITH CONFIDENCE AND FAITH, EACH DO OUR PART AS A TRUSTEE OF EARTH TO TAKE CHARGE AND TAKE CARE OF OUR PLANET.

| *"Christians must be doers of [God's]*
word and not hearers only and . . . they
have an obligation to walk the walk."

People Should Behave Morally to Do God's Will

Sidney Callahan

In the following viewpoint Sidney Callahan presents a Catholic view of ethical behavior. According to Callahan, God desires people to live ethical lives and provides the inspiration to help individuals overcome selfishness and aggressive desires. She defines the Christian path to goodness as one devoted to the will of God. Callahan is a Catholic theologian and a licensed psychologist who has written extensively on religion, psychology, and ethics.

As you read, consider the following questions:

1. What three things does Callahan assert people must have to live an adequate moral or ethical life?
2. According to the author, what does a person need in order to act morally and ethically?
3. What, in Callahan's view, is the only real moral failure possible by Christians?

Sidney Callahan, "Lured by the Spirit to an Ethical Life," *National Catholic Reporter,* vol. 39, December 13, 2002, pp. 32–33. Copyright © 2002 by the *National Catholic Reporter,* www.natcath.org. Reproduced by permission.

W e can be absolutely certain that God is good and wants humankind to be morally upright. The divine mandate for human beings comes through loud and clear in the Ten Commandments, the Golden Rule, and the rest of the scriptures and creeds taught by the church. But Christians may not be so sure of exactly how spirituality and morality relate to each other.

At least we know how scandalous it is when there is a radical disconnect between worship and ethical behavior. Who hasn't been horrified to read of priests sexually abusing children, or nuns abetting genocide, or Catholics taking part in torture or death squads? Clearly in cases of ethical atrocities, religious practice has become separated from the fundamental command to do good and avoid evil.

Yet among ordinary Catholics who are trying to be good, the effort to integrate faith and moral behavior can be a persistent challenge. The faithful recognize that Christians must be doers of the word and not hearers only and that they have an obligation to walk the walk. But how can they live out the gospel in everyday moral living?

An adequate moral or ethical life requires persons to have good hearts, wise heads and virtuous habits of action. Happily, there is little doubt that human beings start out wanting to become good. Always and everywhere children become attached to those who nurture and care for them, and want to gain their approval. Guilt and shame appear very early in human development because children grasp the prevailing standards of morality and achievement and want to meet them.

A Social Species

Human beings are a social species with big brains and the ability to choose between alternative courses of action. Humans can imagine and think about things that are not concretely present. Persons seek meaning as well as love. Evolution innately equips us to seek realities beyond what can be seen.

The innate capacity for the operation of conscience comes from the ability to freely choose between behaviors and the possession of enough intelligence to adopt standards of worth that transcend the self. Wherever humans exist they produce art, music, religion, morality and cultural group norms. All non-impaired adult members of the human species possess a conscience, but Christians identify this powerful ethical pull with the work of the Holy Spirit. God as Spirit may be anonymous and work in hidden ways in the universe, but Christians recognize the One who lures them toward holiness.

Of course, people also possess a selfish drive toward survival that includes competitiveness and the desire for dominance. Hence the universal experience of every individual that they can choose between good and bad deeds. Humankind is basically good but also flawed by being subject to selfish and aggressive desires.

Psychologists now consider that we have been prepared through evolution to have an instantaneous response to events that then can be followed by a more reflective secondary response. The first spontaneous reactions will come from past learning and built-in biological urges for survival; the second response can be guided by new thinking and chosen aspirations or plans for the future. This perceived duality and inner conflict has been the origin of morality and ethics. Their purpose is to help persons to think through choices and resist wrong decisions. Different cultures and different religions will operate in different ways to encourage cooperative moral behavior and discourage actions that destroy human flourishing.

Every known human group possesses moral standards and some form of ethics and some kind of religion. In some instances, members of a social group may not have connected their moral obligations to their kith and kin with their religious beliefs. Religions can exist that are mostly devoted to appeasing supernatural spirits and gaining magic control over nature.

However, in every highly developed universal religion, individual moral behavior is directly related to religious faith and practice. Christianity inherits the genius of the Jewish prophetic tradition that sees true worship of God in love of neighbor, aid to those in need and justice in dealings with others. Traditionally, the church has required that Christians attend worship and practice the 14 corporal and spiritual works of mercy. The final judgment of a Christian life— whether one will be among the sheep or the goats—has been seen to depend upon one's moral behavior toward others.

Practicing Justice

But today in a complicated and highly developed world it is harder to know how to practice justice. It is the institutions and social systems that give us the most moral quandaries. I don't think Christians have too much trouble understanding how their faith applies in private life. Standards of respect and care, shown in word and deed, can be easily applied to one's family, friends, neighbors and colleagues. Honor your old parents, love and be faithful to your spouse, care for children, grandchildren, friends and the neighbor in need. Be honest, don't steal or cheat and strive to keep the Golden Rule.

A more puzzling ethical challenge arises in the matter of deciding an individual's moral responsibility to work for social justice and good institutions. Individualistic Americans resist acknowledging the crucial importance of institutions and social systems. They seem more or less invisible until we bump up against some problematic abuse. We just don't think enough about the way large systems shape our lives. For one thing, such questions can require expert knowledge, and for another the individual can feel helpless to effect change. Re-

Human Laws Versus Divine Laws

"Rules and laws" regulate the formalities of our interactions; they are not a reflection of who, in a deep sense, we as human beings are. They are external to our being; they are a means to our getting along with one another.

It is different with the divine laws. These are an expression of the divine being, and they map what it means to live human lives. When we live in accordance with divine laws, we are fulfilling our calling as human beings. . . . Rules and regulations are a necessary evil; God's law is a positive good.

Miroslav Volf, Christian Century, *February 28, 2001.*

forms may be needed in the church, Congress, tax law, health care, welfare, immigration, education and military policy, but what can we do about it?

The Catholic spiritual tradition offers help in both becoming good as an individual and in deciding what should be done in a larger social context. Whether dealing with individual morality or with larger ethical questions, Catholics are not left alone without resources. There are tried and true ways for Christians to integrate spirituality and moral challenges.

The emotions of charity and empathy are the primary ingredients of moral behavior. If we don't care enough or empathize with others, then we won't see or feel the need to act morally. Evolution has equipped us with an emotional system that works to inform us and galvanize us to action. Emotions make us pay attention to what is going on within us and in the environment. Emotional sensitivity allows us to receive the signals from self and others that point to situations where moral action is needed.

Emotions also help us to think better. Occasionally extreme emotional responses can highjack us and be counterproductive, but in general emotions provide the energizing power to focus our minds. Emotions signal that the matter at hand matters. Love and care are the supreme energizers of the Christian's moral life. So how do we increase in love and beneficence?

Christians are helped to good-heartedness by spending time attending to God's inexhaustible love and mercy toward us and to the world. It is a psychological truth that what we look at, what we desire and love, will slowly shape our image. When Moses spoke with Yahweh, his face became radiant with light. God's promise that with God's people hearts of stone could be replaced with hearts of flesh has been in effect ever since.

Lovers become attuned to one another through the time and attention spent gazing at the other. Mothers and infants get in tune through the same processes of mutual attention. Only a prolonged dialogue with the source of all love and desire can increase our desire. Our fire is enkindled by God's fire.

Transformed Consciousness

Human consciousness flows onward in a dynamic stream and can be gradually transformed by lifting our hearts and minds to God. Prayer, worship and meditation place us in the presence of God's love and enable us to respond and love in a Christ-worthy way.

Christians have been promised that they can become holy by the gift of the Holy Spirit acting within us. We cannot do it alone. The transformation that God works in us is really a matter of being taken into God's family life. As a member of God's family, we begin to take a God's eye view of things. As we increase in loving kindness, we grow more disturbed by the evils that exist within and without. Our own omissions, failures and sins bother us more deeply, and our examinations of conscience become more detailed and subtle. At the same time, the moral evils and sufferings of the world become more upsetting. The desire that God's will be done on earth fuels a healthy kind of moral anger over abuses. So what do we do about it?

Here is where wisdom and good counsel become important in the moral life. It is too simple to ask what would Jesus do—a popular question many people now often hear as WWJD—because we live in different circumstances and have different gifts. Jesus tells us to go and do likewise, so we have to work out what that may mean in our particular case. To act morally and ethically, we need knowledge about ourselves, about the particular case, about the particular context and what would count as a good outcome. Ethics is an art, not a science. Yet choosing moral means to an end is necessary since, as Mahatma Gandhi said, "means are ends in the making."

Facing a moral challenge, whether it be large or small, Christians should pray for guidance. In times of quiet meditation, there is space and time for God's will to emerge in consciousness. Because of the danger of self-deception, it is also important to seek the wisdom and counsel of others. What does the church's social teachings have to say on a particular problem? And what do the wise and good advise?

Humility impels us to gather information and consult others. Individuals engaged in moral decisions need all the help they can get. Even in private individual decisions, consulting others is helpful. Sometimes other people are able to help us see what gifts and talents we possess or lack. The old moral rule that "ought" implies "can" still holds. God does not ask us to do tasks that are beyond our abilities.

Other traditional wisdom about taking account of different states of life is also important. Earlier moral decisions to marry and have children must affect present moral obligations. It's no good deciding to rush off to Calcutta to join Mother Teresa's mission if you will abandon your children, your husband and the dishes. Past professional commitments also affect present ethical choices.

The Assistance of the Holy Spirit

While the specific moral decisions of an individual are her or his own responsibility, the Holy Spirit assists in the operation of conscience. God gives us the perseverance to stick to the hard work involved in a difficult decision. Prudence is doing the best possible thing in the best possible way. Unfortunately, we have seen people do the best possible thing in the worst possible way, the worst possible thing in the best possible way, and so on. Innocent doves can often profit by cultivating the shrewdness of the serpent. Meditating upon God's truth, freedom and power may inspire Christians to more audacious visions of what should be done in a situation. Christians turned the world upside down because they did not adopt the world's view of human possibilities. Christians operate guided by a vision of God's Kingdom, and don't settle for the status quo. With hope and confidence in God, Christians do not have to bow down before the bottom line, or choose to do evil out of some tragic necessity. The only moral failure for Christ's disciples is to abandon the effort to do God's good work. If worldly success follows then that's wonderful, but God's will above all things.

It is good to remember that those persons engaged in the most draining tasks find the strength to keep going by daily prayer and frequent worship. Celebrations of the Christian life enliven and enlighten the human spirit through the power of the Holy Spirit. The more exasperating and frustrating the call to love and justice, the more we need to beg God for fortitude.

Steadfast courage to keep going in the struggle to be good comes from relying on God. The more repetition and drudgery in the duty, the more we need the example of saints and the support of our community. Persecution and conflict can also beset the moral life. Evil persons hate the good and their tranquility. The greatest saints were like Christ in the way that their joy in God's gifts inspired them to make sacrifices for others.

One other law of the moral life helps us on our way. The smallest moral act can bear much fruit. To take one step on the path toward God puts you in a different place with an ability to see further, and seeing more, we can care more deeply. Through caring more we can choose to act again, and yet again. When good choices have been repeated enough times, they become the moral habits we know as virtues. Perhaps one of the delightful ironies of the Holy Spirit's work is that eventually moral behavior becomes second nature. Goodness flows from the joyful heart without struggle or even awareness. At that point, as St. Catherine of Siena has said, all the way to heaven is heaven. We're home free once again.

VIEWPOINT 3

> "We must hand down to future genera-
> tions an inheritance that has not been
> irreparably damaged and polluted."

People Should Behave Ethically for the Good of Future Generations

Federico Mayor Zaragoza

A former director-general of the United Nations Educational, Scientific, and Cultural Organization (UNESCO), Federico Mayor Zaragoza is a biochemist and president of the Foundation for a Culture of Peace. In the following viewpoint, written during his tenure with UNESCO, Zaragoza asserts that those currently alive have a moral obligation to act in ways that will preserve the future of human civilization. He calls on the current generation to adopt a long-term view when problem solving, to prevent the destruction of the environment, and to work toward the continuation of such enduring human values as health, education, equality, freedom, and peace.

As you read, consider the following questions:

1. What was the "new approach" that was undertaken by the United Nations in the aftermath of World War II, according to Zaragoza?

2. In Zaragoza's view, what is the fundamental paradox that shadows progress and civilization?

Federico Mayor Zaragoza, "The Ethics of the Future," *UNESCO Courier,* vol. 51, April 1998, pp. 40–41. Copyright © 1998 by UNESCO. Reproduced by permission.

3. What does the author identify as the "true common heritage of humanity?"

"Our inheritance was not willed to us". With these words, the French poet René Char reminded humanity, amid the ruins of the Second World War, of its basic responsibility towards history. Thus, a generation of survivors took up the cause of future generations.

This new approach, this quest for human solidarity through both space and time, has for over fifty years been the task of the United Nations in general and of UNESCO in particular. "To save succeeding generations from the scourge of war" is the solemn commitment introducing the Charter of the United Nations. This, too, is what is meant by UNESCO's Constitution when it speaks of contributing to peace and security by promoting collaboration among nations through education, science and culture.

The world has, however, changed in the last fifty years, as have the issues, the challenges and, it must be acknowledged, the dangers of modern times. On the eve of the twenty-first century, different wars are breaking out: we have had experience of world wars and bloody conflicts between nations, but today we are witnessing conflicts that tear peoples apart within nations. This is not the place to dwell on other forms of violence: violence against hope and the future of human beings, against their dignity, or the latent conflicts between cultures and between generations. The scourge seems to be universal. All over the world, the citizens of today are claiming rights over the citizens of tomorrow, threatening their well-being and at times their lives. I repeat: today's citizens are claiming rights over tomorrow's, and we are beginning to realize that we are jeopardizing the exercise by future generations of their human rights. More than ever, the ethics of the future requires that we devise and disseminate that culture of peace which was the aim of UNESCO's founders, and see that it is shared.

Limiting the Power of Technology

In the economic and social field, debt, division and instability make up the inglorious heritage, the poisoned legacy we leave to our successors. Look at the earth and the natural environment: gas emissions, desert encroachment, pollution and the misuse of natural resources seem to foredoom the planet. The essential, vital needs of our children, not only the earth, water and air but also knowledge, freedom and solidarity, are being sacrificed on the altar of short-term expediency, ambition and profit, thus encouraging the soft options and selfishness of a short-sighted age, bringing to mind the famous saying attributed to the king of a world on the wane: "Apres moi, le deluge" ["After me, the deluge"].

There are more serious matters still: it is not only society and the environment but the very essence and biological integrity of the human person that are imperiled. It is now within the realms of possibility for humans to modify the genetic heritage of any species, including their own. They even possess the grim privilege of being able to plan their own disappearance. With modern science we have almost reached the point of no return. Never mind the arguments about the compensation in technological or financial terms: there will be no replacement since what is destroyed has no equivalent, and there will be no payout since what is destroyed is without price. Who can compensate for genocide? Who would dare to claim that we can pay for the earth? If we want to protect our descendants, we must first of all recognize, accept and come to terms with this fundamental paradox: progress and civilization are one side of the coin, but the other side is the possibility of an apocalypse, of irreversible destruction, of chaos. A lucid realization of that fact is the prime requirement of our responsibility to future generations. Agreeing to curb the now unbridled power of technology by ethics and wisdom is henceforth the proper course. Lord Acton's dictum that "absolute power corrupts absolutely" needs to be applied to technology,

An Appeal from His Holiness the Dalai Lama

The best way to ensure that when we approach death we do so without remorse is to ensure that in the present moment we conduct ourselves responsibly and with compassion for others. Actually, this is in our own interest, and not just because it will benefit us in the future. . . . Compassion is one of the principal things that make our lives meaningful. It is the source of all lasting happiness and joy. And it is the foundation of a good heart, the heart of one who acts out of a desire to help others. Through kindness, through affection, through honesty, through truth and justice toward all others we ensure our own benefit. This is not a matter for complicated theorizing. It is a matter of common sense. There is no denying that consideration of others is worthwhile. There is no denying that our happiness is inextricably bound up with the happiness of others. There is no denying that if society suffers, we ourselves suffer. Nor is there any denying that the more our hearts and minds are afflicted with ill-will, the more miserable we become. Thus we can reject everything else: religion, ideology, all received wisdom. But we cannot escape the necessity of love and compassion.

The Dalai Lama, Ethics for the New Millennium, *1999.*

while science needs to be reminded of [François] Rabelais' saying that "science without conscience is but ruination of the soul".

But where does science dwell, and where are we to look for wisdom? We are nowadays able to travel to the other end of the earth in a matter of hours, and we are able to see for ourselves that, while the great cities of the industrialized countries may possess the knowledge, it is in the remotest villages that the wisdom is to be found. . . . We at last have the ability to reconcile knowledge and wisdom and to make them benefit from each other's virtues. With this in mind, we in UNESCO drew up, with the assistance of the International Bioethics Committee, the Universal Declaration on the Human Genome and Human Rights which was adopted by the Organization's General Conference in November [1997]—the first universal declaration to apply to science and to lay down ethical principles in this field which will remind us all that we are born free and equal.

Foreseeing in Order to Build

I said we must—in the name of ethics and wisdom—agree to curb the power that technology gives to humans over humans. The issue looms large and the challenge is a real one. In an age of globalization and of the acceleration and multiplication of exchanges, the future appears, if not dark, then at least unclear. Complexity and uncertainty are the key words of our time. I therefore invoke the virtues of an education of concern, since concern stirs us to action, whereas conformity and optimism benumb us. This is, of course, to assume willingness on our part to observe and ask questions of the future, for our temporal short-sightedness is often coupled with a willful blindness, when not serving as a justification for it. Caught in the whirl of the quick fix, held in the tyrannical grip of short-termism, we do not take the time to shape our actions or think about their consequences. We are hurtling into the future with no brakes and in conditions of zero visibility. But the faster a car goes, the brighter its headlights must be: it is no longer, therefore, a question of adjusting or adapting—adjustment and adaptation always lag behind events, which move ahead more rapidly—but a matter of taking preemptive action. We should stop talking about adjustment and adaptation and take a clear-sighted, forward-looking approach, casting a future-oriented eye on the world. We should plant today

the seeds of tomorrow, protecting them as they grow, so that tomorrow our children may harvest the fruits of our foresight. To foresee in order to prevent and to foresee in order to build—these are our objectives.

Preserving the Human Element

Prevention is not merely a possibility: it is an obligation and a moral imperative. This idea has indeed already made some headway in public awareness and in international law. It has even given rise to a new principle, enshrined in 1992 at the Earth Summit in Rio [de Janeiro] and incorporated into the Maastricht Treaty [creating the European Union] and some national standard-setting instruments: I refer to the precautionary principle. But the view of that principle which has prevailed has been that of a principle of inaction rather than one of vigilant action. Risk-taking without knowledge is dangerous, but knowledge without risk-taking is worthless. Today, alas, more than five years after the Rio Summit, what has been the outcome, where are the results? The commitments then made have given way to evasiveness, and Agenda 21 [to protect the environment] has to all intents and purposes remained a dead letter. "Rio plus 5" is "Rio minus 5". We have to ponder this lesson, and sow within democracy itself the seed that can revitalize and reconstitute it. That seed is and can only be the ethics of the future, made central to decision-making, central to democratic deliberation, central to the kind of adversarial appraisal that, rather than obfuscating, appeasing or misleading opinion by serving vested interests, the authorities and the powers that be, must enlighten the public and form its judgement.

Prevention means first and foremost preserving. The ethics of the future is an ethics of the fragile and the perishable. We must hand down to future generations an inheritance that has not been irreparably damaged and polluted. We must bequeath to them the right to live in a world preserved. This

107

concerns first of all our living environment—the new preoccupation of the present age—and such enduring values as health, education, culture, equality, freedom, peace, tolerance and solidarity. The Catalan poet Salvador Espriu told his children: "I have lived to preserve these few words which I bequeath to you: love, justice and freedom". We are responsible not only for our tangible heritage; the essential objects of our duty and responsibility are often invisible and intangible. The concept of heritage has thus taken on new meanings in recent decades: from the straightforward preservation of historic monuments to the Convention for the Protection of the World Cultural and Natural Heritage, adopted in 1972, and from the recognition of our non-material, symbolic and spiritual heritage to the work currently being done by the International Bioethics Committee on the protection of the human genome, the concept of being has gradually pervaded that of having. It is human beings themselves who are the true common heritage of humanity, our priceless universal birthright.

At the dawn of a new century and a new millennium, at a time when the global village no longer seems so distant a prospect, we must shoulder our responsibilities as citizens of the world. This means that we must become aware of our position, in human history as well as in space, and must reflect on our role on the planet and in history. One's love for one's neighbour is indeed also to be measured by the respect one shows for those far distant. Near or far, yesterday or today, other people are still our fellow creatures. Both in space and in time, humanity is one body and we are its members.

> "The point of all [government] ethics systems is to reinforce the public's confidence in the institutions of government."

Government Employees Must Behave Ethically to Preserve Democracy

Stuart C. Gilman

Stuart C. Gilman worked in the federal government's Office of Government Ethics and was president of the Ethics Resource Center before being named program director for the United Nations Global Programme Against Corruption in 2005. In the following viewpoint Gilman emphasizes the importance of government ethics in a democracy, noting that without the confidence of the governed, government institutions lose their legitimacy. Although the United States employs many methods for ensuring ethical conduct at all levels of government, Gilman argues that other democracies, such as Australia, Canada and New Zealand, do a better job of making sure that public officials behave ethically. Rather than publish rules for officials to follow, which is what America does, these nations define the values and attributes that public employees should embrace.

Stuart C. Gilman, "Government Ethics: If Only Angels Were to Govern," *Phi Kappa Phi Forum*, vol. 83, Spring 2003. Copyright © 2003 by Stuart C. Gilman. Reproduced by permission of the publisher.

As you read, consider the following questions:

1. In Gilman's opinion, what positive outcomes are achieved through the federal government's ethics system?

2. Why, in the author's opinion, are state and local government officials among the most vulnerable to conflicts of interest?

3. According to Gilman, why would a values-based system of government ethics be better for the United States?

I f angels were to govern men, neither external nor internal controls on Government would be necessary. In framing a Government which is to be administered by men over men, the great difficulty lies in this: you must first enable the Government to control the governed; and in the next place oblige it to control itself. A dependence on the people is, no doubt, the primary control on the Government; but experience has taught mankind the necessity of auxiliary precautions.

—*James Madison, Federalist Papers #51 (1787)*

Democratic government is always fragile. Yet democratic government is something most Americans take for granted. Through skill, luck, insight, tinkering, and persistence, the United States has become one of the strongest models for democracy in the world. Certainly, geography, natural resources, and the diversity of its people have contributed to this success. However, we often ignore the institutional fabric and the ethical values and structures that undergird the great American democratic experiment.

For the average citizen, the term "ethics," including government ethics, seems abstract. Punsters even suggest that it is an oxymoron. The reality is quite different. Since the 1970s, ethics systems have become dominant at both federal and state levels in the United States and to some degree have become models for the rest of the world. However, by and large, the systems have little to do with imparting values and fundamental ethical principles. Instead, government ethics systems emphasize compliance with laws and regulations. And, the vast majority of these laws and regulations focuses on conflicts of interest.

These legal structures are often based on fundamental principles, codes of ethics, and codes of conduct. However, often little ties the aspirational values in these codes or principles to what is often overly complex legal guidance. For the most part, government ethics is currently a list of "don'ts" with very little explanation as to why government officials should do the right thing. Often, the most complex of legal discussions obscures even the "don'ts." This having been said, our surveying this landscape of government ethics to understand both its potential for guiding ethical conduct and the lurking ethical problems that still confront us as a democratic society is a worthwhile endeavor. The point of all ethics systems is to reinforce the public's confidence in the institutions of government. If such systems fail at this purpose, they are paper structures that can actually increase the public's cynicism.

Government Ethics

Until the Watergate scandal [1972–74], government ethics was a hodgepodge of rules and regulations that forbade certain forms of conduct without a reasonable framework or institutions to provide advice or enforcement. However, Watergate was the turning point for ethics in the United States. In 1978, the government sought to implement a compliance-based approach to ethics to prevent the gross misconduct that had occurred during Watergate—when government ethics had not yet been defined—by passing new legislation (such as post-employment restrictions) and creating several new institutions. Within months of each other, the federal government created the first six inspectors general (there are now more than sixty), the provision for appointing Independent Counsels . . . , the Office of Special Counsel (to protect whistleblowers), the Federal Election Commission, and finally the Office of Government Ethics to provide interpretation, guidance, financial disclosure, and education on the ethical obligations of all employees.

The U.S. government's own reforms of government ethics implemented in 1978 were designed to be both carrot and stick: some institutions were created to provide guidance and protection for those who did the right thing, and other institutions were created to ensure effective punishment if laws or rules were violated. The success of these institutions can be debated; however, it would be a mistake to believe that a heavily compliance-based system is the only way to have government ethics—because, as complex as the U.S. system is, it has not had the success of countries such as Australia, Canada, and New Zealand, where codes of ethics are based on clear and simple positive attributes. In these countries, regulations are minimal and encourage values-based behavior rather than simply compliance with rules. Enforcement, especially for administrative infractions, can be broadly based (for example, for an action that has undermined the integrity of the public service).

The Federal Government

Our federal government has implemented ethics in several layers, as noted above. Congress established the U.S. Office of Government Ethics (OGE) as a decentralized system. More than one hundred designated Directors of Agency Ethics Offices (DAEOs), who head ethics offices in every government agency, now exist. DAEOs serve several functions: to provide counseling, advice, and training, and to administer a financial-disclosure system. (A single code of conduct as well as massive training on ethics was implemented by the Office of Government Ethics pursuant to Executive Order 12674 by President George H. W. Bush in 1989.) Under this executive order, a

Standards of Ethical Conduct for Employees of the Executive Branch of the U.S. Government

1. Public service is a public trust, requiring employees to place loyalty to the Constitution, the laws and ethical principles above private gain.

2. Employees shall not hold financial interests that conflict with the conscientious performance of duty.

3. Employees shall not engage in financial transactions using nonpublic Government information or allow the improper use of such information to further any private interest.

4. An employee shall not . . . solicit or accept any gift or other item of monetary value from any person or entity seeking official action from, doing business with, or conducting activities regulated by the employee's agency, or whose interests may be substantially affected by the performance or nonperformance of the employee's duties. . . .

U.S. Office of Government Ethics, "Standards of Ethical Conduct for Employees of the Executive Branch," October 2, 2002.

single, comprehensive Code of Conduct was created for the executive branch, as well as education requirements, including annual training for the most senior executive-branch employees.

Perhaps the most controversial program overseen by the OGE is collecting, evaluating, and releasing financial-disclosure forms for 20,000 of the most senior government officials. These individuals are required to list the assets, liabilities, agreements, boards, and commitments for themselves, their spouses, and their minor children. If the individual is a political appointee, the public financial disclosure must be submitted to OGE before the appointee's Senate confirmation hearing. The disclosure is "scrubbed" by agency officials and OGE to remove any real or potential ethical problems. According to OGE unofficial estimates, nearly one-third of all political appointees are required to make some changes before their hearing, indicating that without some government oversight there would be many unrecognized or unknown conflicts of interest.

Senior civil servants and ambassadors, as well as generals and admirals, must file the same form when they assume their posts. The OGE and/or the agency's ethics official reviews all forms and advises candidates on how to divest certain assets to avoid potential conflicts of interest, either through the sale of some assets, not participating in certain activities, or putting assets into a blind trust. All of the twenty-some-thousand government employees must file a disclosure when they enter office, annually while in office, and when they leave office. In addition, more than 200,000 confidential-disclosure filers must file similar forms that are not available to the public.

This system has many drawbacks. It is burdensome. The large number of individuals required to file is out of proportion to the actual number of people in which the public and the press are really interested. It duplicates, for many political appointees, similar forms required by individual Senate committees responsible for confirmation. For that reason, it is considered one more impediment to public service for those who want to serve. The system is far from perfect, but it does identify problems, focus public servants on their ethical responsibilities, and discourage those who would try to abuse public office from filling government positions. Ultimately, the question is one of balance. It is a continuing question that we will wrestle with in public-policy circles for the foreseeable future.

The States

The individual states have vastly different systems of government ethics. Some states require only financial disclosure by personnel; others involve themselves only in the election process; some oversee multiple county commissions; others have implemented codes of conduct; and some directly intervene during cases of prosecution. States truly are the laboratories of democracy when it comes to ethics. In all, there are some forty state ethics commissions and more than a dozen ethics offices in metropolitan areas, plus perhaps hundreds of local and county ethics offices. State ethics commissions vary widely in their political strength: in New Jersey, the legislature designed the ethics office to be weak; in Missouri and Virginia, despite legislative mandates, the ethics offices have proven ineffective and have actually "disappeared" from time to time; in Wisconsin, the Ethics Board has played a strong role in enforcing its code of conduct and in anticipating possible ethical dilemmas; in Alabama, a strong ethics commission has not been afraid to take on the governor if necessary.

Areas of Vulnerability

Congress Although both houses of Congress have ethics committees with sophisticated staff members, they are significantly limited because of the perceived politics of ethics accusations. In the late 1970s the original design of the congressional ethics system required the Government Accounting Office (GAO) to do oversight. The GAO was far too intrusive for many members of Congress, which has led to the current system. The dilemma is that the ethical expectations for representatives and senators are constantly changing, leading to what one scholar has called "mediated political corruption." Fair or not, it is the reality that representatives and senators face. Ironically, many in Congress seem to feel license in the area of ethics and to be insensitive to the concerns of the public. One can make a reasonable claim that the Founders in writing the Constitution saw the Congress as an inherent bundle of conflicts of interest. Apparently, few in Congress today feel the tension caused by these conflicts.

Just this year [2003] the House of Representatives liberalized rules on accepting meals and gifts for themselves and their staffs. This area has always been troublesome, and many in Congress seem willing to increase the vulnerability of the institution for the price of a meal. The House of Representatives is especially vulnerable to these kinds of ethics failings. For the past five years, the House has been operating under an ethics truce. Recently, when Ethics committee Democrats suggested that Representative Martin Oxley be investigated, the Republicans threatened that they would then demand an investigation of Democratic Representative Nancy Pelosi. This bizarre stalemate appears to set the stage for an unprecedented scandal in the future. It is too strong to suggest that this system is bankrupt, but it is far too limited to prevent abuse.

State Legislatures At the state level, legislators face additional ethical vulnerabilities. Because most state legislators are only part-time, they are confronted with a host of conflicts of interest. Yet, there is little ethics oversight of state legislators' activities and almost no training or education to sensitize them to the ethical issues that they confront. If we are to have "citizen-legislators," then we owe them the protections afforded through clear guidance and serious ethical education. It is both naive and dangerous to assume that everyone knows "ethics" or that elections make legislators wise in this area. For that reason, state legislators and local council members are some of the most ethically vulnerable people in government.

The Judiciary Equally as worrisome is the ethical situation of the judiciary in the United States. At the federal level, justices are protected from some types of conflicts of interest through their lifetime appointments. Yet this same protection makes them insensitive to at least the appearance of conflicts of interest. It is common for federal judges to accept free trips for "seminars" to exotic places from a variety of sources, including plaintiffs who have appeared (or will appear) before them.

Many Americans do not realize that most state judges are elected. A recent study by the Committee for Economic Development noted that almost 27,000 of the 30,000 non-federal judges are elected in the United States. In thirty-nine of the fifty states, some or all of the judges are elected. In the past, this method has not been a problem. However, recently, trial lawyers and corporations have competed to seat judges favorable to their points of view, from trial judges all the way to state supreme courts. The cost of these elections has gone up dramatically, so that the rather bizarre specter of trial judges raising campaign contributions in their courtroom has become a reality. . . . The only possible results from these mammoth infusions of money in judicial elections are either actual corruption of judges or a perception that justice can be bought. Arguably, the latter, absent any real conflicts, could do the most damage to our civil- and criminal-justice systems. This is a scandal waiting to be born.

The Executive The executive branch, with all its sophisticated ethics apparati, still has a significant number of vulnerabilities. Governments at all levels are geometrically increasing the amount of privatization and "contracting out." The reality is that many agencies are left with skeleton management teams who have little competence to oversee the contracts for which they are responsible. Even worse, many functions that were formerly considered inherently governmental have been contracted out. One can argue that several elements of U.S. foreign and domestic policy-making have actually been "contracted." Finally, political appointees are paid relatively little compared with their private sector counterparts, leaving room for temptation, perceived conflicts of interest, and out-and-out corruption. Although pressure has been brought to bear from all areas of the government to reduce the complexity of ethics oversight, it would be naive to suggest that there are no continuing vulnerabilities in the executive branches of government, both political and civil service, from the council chamber to the presidency.

The Good Government

Because the United States has shied away from a values system for ethical behavior in the government, employees often find very fine distinctions between good conduct and misconduct. The tendency for many public servants is to ask whether an action violates the law, rather than if it is the behavior that the American people expect from their public servants. Even though the United States has one of the most sophisticated systems of government ethics, it is also one of the most complex and dynamic. Because many systems are rule-bound, it has actually become more difficult to determine when someone has violated them. The research of the Ethics Resource Center, as well as international models provided by Canada, Australia, New Zealand, and England, suggests that the American public would be better served by a values-based system for public servants. Such a program would emphasize the positive values of public service and provide a clear vision of the obligations that Americans expect from those who work for them.

More than a thousand years ago a great Chinese sage is credited with the following aphorism that captures the essence of my argument:

Tzu Kung asked for a definition of good government. The Master replied: It consists in providing enough food to eat, in keeping enough soldiers to guard the State, and in winning the confidence of the people.—And if one of these three things had to be sacrificed, which should go first?—The Master replied: Sacrifice the soldiers.—And if of the two remaining things one had to be sacrificed, which should it be?—The Master replied: let it be the food. From the beginning men have always had to die. But without the confidence of the people no government can stand at all.

> *"If we want to raise ethical children, we have no choice but to work on developing our character."*

Adults Should Behave Morally to Be Good Role Models for Children

Lawrence Kelemen

Lawrence Kelemen is a professor of education at Neve Yerushalayim College of Jewish Studies for Women in Jerusalem, Israel. He lectures throughout North and South America, Europe, and the Middle East, and is the author of several books on education and parenting. In the following viewpoint Kelemen asserts that in order to teach ethical behavior to children, adults should continually work to improve their own behavior. According to Kelemen, children imitate the behaviors that are modeled for them by adults and will grow up to act in ways that are very similar to the adults in their lives. Therefore, Kelemen asserts that parents and teachers who hope to be positive role models for children should focus their efforts on developing their own characters.

As you read, consider the following questions:

1. As related by Kelemen, researchers believe newborn humans begin imitating adult behavior at what age?

2. What is a *vaad*, as defined by the author?

3. What are the two inheritances that parents attempt to pass on to their children, according to Kelemen?

I f we want to raise ethical children, we have no choice but to work on developing our character.

When asked about the greatest challenge he faces today, the principal of one of the largest Jewish high schools in the United States related to me this complaint:

> Parents spend thousands of dollars a year in tuition to send their children to our school where, along with calculus and chemistry, we are expected to teach some semblance of ethics. Then, on Sunday, the parents take their child to an amusement park and lie about his age in order to save five dollars on the admission fee. To save five bucks they destroy a $15,000 education.

Our best day school and high school principals have included separate ethics courses in their school curricula. A handful of these educational experts have gone even further, weaving an ethics perspective into every aspect of their schools' educational program. All of these curricular and extra-curricular programs constitute heroic attempts to provide our children with the highest quality Jewish education. It is hard to imagine what more the brave pioneers of these programs can do to improve our children's character.

There is another step we could take, and that step might do more to improve our children's ethics than any of the commendable efforts described above. We parents and teachers could also engage in the sort of structured and guided work on character development we are so proud to see our children do. We could create "mussar vaadim" (ongoing character-development workshops) for interested parents and teachers. Participants in these programs would actively work on their character so as to be more thoroughly refined models for their students.

Religion and Psychology Agree on the Importance of Role Models

Our tradition tells us that we parents and teachers can be powerful role models. The rabbis of the Talmud long ago explained, for example, that a child speaks in the marketplace the way he heard his parents speaking at home. Psychologists also remind us that the model we parents present influences even our youngest children.

Consider this report from the *Journal of the American Medical Association [JAMA]*:

> Neonates are born with an instinctive capacity and desire to imitate adult human behavior. That infants can, and do, imitate an array of adult facial expressions has been demonstrated in neonates as young as a few hours old, i.e., before they are even old enough to know cognitively that they themselves have facial features that correspond with those they are observing. It is a most useful instinct, for the developing child must learn and master a vast repertoire of behavior in short order.

The *JAMA* report also warns about the downside of pediatric modeling:

> Whereas infants have an instinctive desire to imitate observed human behavior, they do not possess an instinct for gauging a priori whether a behavior ought to be imitated. They will imitate almost anything, including behaviors that most adults would regard as destructive and antisocial.

U.S. studies indicate that the probability of a child's smoking doubles if one parent smokes and quadruples if both parents smoke. Data from the Norwegian National Health Survey

Establishing Ethical Behavior in Children

We tend to think that requiring our kids to do things will make them hate those things, but in fact requiring altruistic behavior, as part of family and community projects, creates habits that resurface later. I emphasize family and community because children learn a lot more from watching than they do from listening. "Do as I say, not as I do" has never worked. . . .

Values are transmitted to the next generation if they're a part of the varied fabric of a community, part of not only lessons and lectures, but also songs, plays, stories, traditions, and rituals. . . . All the research says that if you want your values to be passed on, you have to do more than talk about them. You have to explore and celebrate them in as many ways as you can think of. And you have to act on them, visibly and continually, inside as well as outside.

Kate Lovelady, "Ethics: The Next Generation,"
New York Society for Ethical Culture,
October 3, 2004. www.nysec.org.

demonstrate that the probability of a young adult's having a diet low in fat is five times higher if one of his parents had a low fat intake. Similar associations exist for alcohol consumption, wearing seatbelts and doing exercise, and we have no reason to believe parental example does not powerfully influence all behaviors.

If we respond to disobedience harshly, our children and students will likely do the same. If we are dishonest or steal, the odds are that our children will internalize these behaviors too. Whether or not we intend to do so, through example we plant our own behavior in our children. Unless they make heroic efforts to uproot these seeds later in life, our children will grow up to be very much like us.

The Example of an Honest Parent

Of course, we parents can also be the most powerful positive role models in our children's lives. A mother whose child attends a yeshiva [Jewish] high school told me this story:

She went to the market with her children. When she was checking out, the clerk failed to properly credit her for a promotional item. After unsuccessfully trying to rectify the matter with the checkout clerk, the woman approached the store manager and explained the mistake. The manager was busy, not terribly interested in the woman's complaint, and initially uncooperative. However, eventually the manager reached into his cash drawer and handed her two dollars compensation. On their way home, the woman realized that the manager had given her too much money. She was already late, however, and could not return to the market.

That night, however, the woman could not sleep. She kept thinking about the money in her wallet that did not belong to her. In the morning, she rushed the children to get ready for school early, left with them ahead of schedule, and drove straight to the market. There, in front of her children, she explained to the manager the mistake he had made the previous day. The manager was not interested in the story but took the overpayment and returned it to the register drawer.

Months later, the woman's son took a difficult test at school. Most students did poorly on the test, but her child received a mark of "A+". Indeed, in front of the class the teacher praised the boy for his perfect performance. Then, because so many students had received low grades, the teacher decided to review the correct answers aloud with the class. During the review, the boy realized that he had actually made a mistake on the exam but the teacher had failed to see it. Throughout the review the boy struggled with his desire for the "A+". Ultimately his conscience triumphed. After class he approached the teacher and pointed out the grading error.

At home later that day, the boy told his mother the story. She praised him for his willingness to sacrifice his "A+" on the altar of honesty. Her son explained that a battle had raged inside of him while he listened to the review. But then he remembered his distraught mother trying to give some cash back to a market manager. The boy told his mother that in that moment his internal battle ended and he realized what he was going to do. (As a pleasant postscript to the story: The teacher was so impressed with the boy's honesty, she rewarded him by giving him the "A+" despite the mistake.)

The Challenge of Adult Character Development

We all know of children who have been scarred by parents and teachers who respond with anger, use vicious language, or display selfishness, dishonesty, or other less-than-refined traits. Sometimes they drop their religiosity. Sometimes they just mirror the harshness they experienced at home or in the classroom. I meet such children every week. They are living testimony to the necessity of a formal framework for adult character development.

Most parents and teachers realize that values and perspectives must be planted by personal example. However, in practice we sometimes try to build into our children and students behavioral routines that we personally have not yet mastered. We insist that our children get proper sleep, even though we scrape by on far less than we need. We insist that they eat properly, even though we survive on coffee and donuts. We insist that they control their anger, even though we sometimes show rage. In short, we find it easier to work on our children than on ourselves, and so that is sometimes what we do.

This hypocrisy has disastrous results: Too many children legitimately view their parents and/or teachers as insincere. Disrespect burgeons slowly until, around ages 12–15, it shreds the parent-child or teacher-student relationship. Then children reject the moral authority of the adults in their lives. They isolate themselves emotionally from parents and teachers, and begin making their own (often self-destructive) decisions.

Or sometimes these children thoroughly accept the lessons of their childhood. They might behave beautifully and do well in school, but they also absorb their mentors' inconsistency. By their late teens or early twenties, these children have mastered the art of hypocrisy, and much of their behavior has absolutely nothing to do with their stated values. These are the university-age students who claim they want a better world and yet purchase term papers off the Internet. Even if we never cheated in school, if we acted with hypocrisy in other areas of our lives, our children will absorb that lesson and practice it wholesale.

Eventually, the real values and perspectives we parents and teachers planted through our own behavior (for better or worse) show themselves. If we want to raise children who will grow into good adults, we must plant the seeds of goodness with our own sterling conduct.

Being a model is not easy. Our children see us at all hours of the day under all circumstances, making it impossible to maintain a facade of ethical refinement. If we have a temper or other negative traits, they will see these. Moreover, as we struggle to behave appropriately at all times, we discover that good intentions alone do not produce good behavior. Sometimes, even when we do not want to get angry, we find ourselves slipping out of control. We have no choice but to work on ourselves. We must set aside time to develop our character, especially our patience.

The Jewish Tradition of Character Development

The traditional framework for working on character is the vaad—a group of five to 15 people, led by a Torah scholar experienced in vaad work. This traditional approach is complex, long-term, often counterintuitive, and highly effective. Here in Jerusalem there are over 120 English-speaking mothers and fathers participating in *vaads,* ongoing character-development workshops. Most have been members of their *vaad* for more than four years, and many have participated for over seven years. They meet every 2–6 weeks to learn about the particular character trait they are working on, receive practical exercises and readings that will help internalize the character trait, and discuss their successes and failures.

I saw members of one *vaad* work on themselves until anger became an extremely rare and muted event. I saw members of another *vaad* develop so much integrity that members never broke their word, even when the commitment was as small as "I'll be off the phone in a minute." These are great achievements, and they have exerted profound influence on the *vaad* members' children (some of whom are in their late teens and early twenties and have joined *vaads* themselves).

Jewish education has come a long way in the last 50 years, and the Jewish day school movement has consistently been on the cutting edge of this progress. Perhaps the time has come to redefine the state-of-the-art in Jewish education, and perhaps innovative day school administrators, teachers, and parents will once again lead the way.

Character and Faith

When our forefather Abraham sent his servant Eliezer off to find a wife for his son, Isaac, Abraham asked Eliezer to swear that he wouldn't bring home a woman from the local Canaanites—known for being murderers and thieves. Rather, Eliezer was told to select a woman from Abraham's homeland—even though those women were known for being idol worshippers.

The author of the Torah commentary, Kli Yakar, asks why Abraham preferred an idol worshipper over a murderer or thief. He answers that although we parents attempt to pass two inheritances to the next generation—our character traits and our beliefs—only our character traits pass instantly and without modification into our children. Our beliefs hover in spiritual no-man's-land until our children choose to accept them or reject them.

Abraham understood that murder and theft result from corrupt character. He reasoned that a woman from a family with corrupt traits would necessarily pass those traits on to her children, and the Jewish People would need to make a massive effort in later generations to clean out this character-contamination. Idol worship, in contrast, results from mistaken beliefs. Unlike the inheritance of character traits, parental beliefs don't necessarily penetrate too deeply and their superficial influence could be corrected quickly. As long as the character traits of Isaac's future wife were in order, a few introduction-to-Judaism classes could straighten out her beliefs, and her descendents then would be refined, faithful members of the Jewish nation.

Jewish day school administrators, teachers, and parents now have an extraordinary opportunity to guarantee the inheritance of our children. The character-development *vaad* has proven popular here in Jerusalem. Without doubt, it would be at least as popular in other cities across the world. Perhaps ongoing character-development workshops are the framework we will choose to build the spiritual fortune we will pass to the next generation.

Periodical Bibliography

The following articles have been selected to supplement the diverse views presented in this chapter.

Jean Brown	"Giving Hope to Humanity: Step Four to Remaking the World," *For a Change*, August/September 2005.
Charles Colson	"Law Isn't Enough," *Washington Post*, July 30, 2002.
David P. Gushee	"Our Missing Moral Compass: Christianity Is More than an Event, an Experience, or a Set of Beliefs," *Christianity Today*, November 2005.
Garret Keizer	"Left, Right, and Wrong: What's Missing from the Debate over Values in America," *Mother Jones*, March/April 2005.
Elizabeth K. Kellar	"12 Steps for Ethical Leadership," *Public Management*, November 2005.
Janelle Lazzo	"Heaven, Self-Respect, and the Golden Rule: Diverse Group Contemplates Reasons to Be Good," *National Catholic Reporter*, December 13, 2002.
Joe Lieberman	"Vision for America: A Place for Faith," *Responsive Community*, Winter 2000–2001.
William Schweiker	"A Preface to Ethics: Global Dynamics and the Integrity of Life," *Journal of Religious Ethics*, Spring 2004.
Brian Starks and Robert V. Robinson	"Who Values the Obedient Child Now? The Religious Factor in Adult Values for Children, 1986–2002," *Social Forces*, September 2005.
David M. Walker	"Ethics and Integrity in Government: Putting the Needs of Our Nation First," *Public Manager*, Summer 2005.

CHAPTER 3

Are Modern Biomedical Practices Ethical?

Chapter Preface

To live a long and healthy life, to be free from suffering, and to die peacefully are universal human concerns. Throughout history, medical and scientific researchers have pursued these goals, and in the twentieth century enormous gains were made in understanding the processes that bring forth life, improve its quality, and prolong it. Since the 1970s, medicine and science have assisted in the creation of life through such technologies as in vitro fertilization. Advancements in curing diseases and prolonging life have likewise developed through pharmacological, surgical, and mechanical means. To be sure, the technologies, procedures, and medicines that can be brought to bear on almost any medical condition in the early twenty-first century is staggering. Yet learning that something can be done is often only part of the work that scientists must engage in. Biomedical ethics seeks to answer as well whether a thing *ought* to be done. Often, as in the case of assisted reproductive technologies and embryonic stem cell research, this means weighing the potential negative consequences of a procedure against its benefits.

The birth of the first "test tube" baby in 1978 was a milestone in the development of reproductive technologies. However, even decades after this breakthrough, some critics continue to challenge the assumption that assisted reproductive technologies (ART) are ethical. Those who question the use of such technologies find the number of unused or destroyed embryos unacceptable. They also point out the risks of birth defects to children conceived through ART as well as the additional medical hazards faced by babies conceived through these means. Others, however, defend ART, asserting that medicine has a moral obligation to help people who have difficulty conceiving naturally.

In addition, ethical questions continue to shadow the disposition of the human embryos that are conceived through ART. Many scientists believe that embryonic stem cell research, which involves removing stem cells from early stage human embryos and then transforming the cells into other cell types, may lead to new ways to fight disease. However, removing the stem cells destroys the embryos (which are obtained from clinics engaging in ART). Proponents of such research cite the potential benefits to patients with debilitating illnesses as the greater good. They assert that since saving human lives is universally considered a moral good, then embryonic stem cell research is by definition ethical. Yet since human embryonic cells cannot be classified as anything other than *human*, their very essence, according to opponents of embryonic stem cell research, affords them the highest protection. These analysts contend that embryos should therefore not be used experimentally regardless of the purpose of the research.

As the debates over ART and embryonic stem cell research show, determining whether or not a particular medical technology is ethical can be enormously challenging. The difficulty resides in the often conflicting goals inherent in creating, improving, and prolonging human life. As German physician and Theologian Albert Schweitzer once said, "Let me give you one definition of ethics: It is good to maintain life and to further life; it is bad to damage and destroy life. And this ethic, profound, universal, has the significance of a religion. It is religion." While seemingly clear advice to guide doctors and scientists in making moral decisions, it is clear that his words also contain a conundrum. In the pursuit of furthering life, researchers often destroy it, as can be seen with ART and embryonic stem cell research. The authors in the following chapter continue the debate over whether modern biomedical procedures are ethical.

> "We may soon learn to direct [embryonic stem cells] to become vehicles of lifesaving potential."

Embryonic Stem Cell Research Is Ethical

Michael D. West

Michael D. West contends in the following viewpoint that no one can say for sure that using embryos for research is tantamount to killing human life because scientists have not proven when life begins. Moreover, he claims that embryonic stem cells—which can be coaxed to become many different kinds of cells and tissues—could be used to cure human diseases. Because embryonic stem cell research could save human lives, he argues, society has an ethical obligation to support it. Michael West is president, chairman, and CEO of Advanced Cell Technology, Inc., a biotechnology company developing potential medical applications of cloning and embryonic stem cell technologies.

As you read, consider the following questions:

1. According to West, how are Siamese twins created?
2. How might scientists solve the problem of histocompatibility, as stated by the author?
3. How does West define teleological and deontological arguments?

Michael D. West, testimony before the U.S. Senate Subcommittee on Labor, Health and Human Services, and Education, Committee on Appropriations, Washington, DC, July 18, 2001.

I am pleased to testify today in regard to the new opportunities and challenges associated with human embryonic stem (ES) cell and nuclear transfer (NT) [cloning] technologies. I will begin by describing the bright promise of these twin and interrelated technologies and then attempt to correct some misunderstandings relating to their application in medicine.

It may be useful to point out that I think of myself as pro-life in that I have an enormous respect for the value of the individual human life. Indeed, in my years following college I joined others in the protest of abortion clinics. My goal was not to send a message to women that they did not have the right to choose. My intent was simply to urge them to reconsider the destruction of a developing human being. Despite my strong convictions about the value of the individual human life, in 1995 I organized the collaboration between [biopharmaceutical] Geron Corporation and the laboratories of Drs. James Thomson and John Gearhart [both holders of U.S.-approved patents for human embryonic stem cell lines] to isolate embryonic stem cells and human embryonic germ cells from human embryos and fetuses respectively. My reasons were simple. These technologies are entirely designed to be used in medicine to alleviate human suffering and to save human life. They are, in fact, pro-life. The opponents that argue they destroy human lives are simply and tragically mistaken. Let me explain why this is the case.

When Human Life Begins

We are composed of trillions of individual living cells, glued together like the bricks of a building to construct the organs and tissues of our body. The cells in our bodies are called "somatic cells" to distinguish them from the "germ line", that is, the reproductive cells that connect the generations. We now know that life evolved from such single-celled organisms that dominated all life some one billion years ago.

"It Is Immoral to Ban Human Cloning"

One can argue about the status of a fetus in the late stages of pregnancy, but there are no rational grounds for ascribing rights to a clump of cells in a Petri dish. It is irrelevant that those cells may have the potential, if implanted in a womb, to produce a baby. A potentiality is not an actuality. . . .

The idea of banning such research to sacrifice actual lives to potential ones is obscenely wrong—wrong morally and politically.

Harry Binswanger, Herald Sun *(Australia),*
January 7, 2004. www.aynrand.org.

Therefore, in answer to the question of when life begins, we must make a crucial distinction. Biological life, that is to say, "cellular life" has no recent beginnings. Our cells are, in fact, the descendents of cells that trace their beginnings to the origin of life on earth. However, when we speak of an individual human life, we are speaking of the communal life of a multicellular organism springing from the reproductive lineage of cells. The individual human life is a body composed of cells committed to somatic cell lineages. All somatic cells are related in that they originate from an original cell formed from the union of a sperm and egg cell.

The fertilization of the egg cell by a sperm leads to a single cell called the "zygote". From this first cell, multiple rounds of cell division over the first week result in a microscopic ball of cells with very unusual properties. This early embryo, called the "preimplantation embryo", has not implanted in the uterus to begin a pregnancy. It is estimated that approximately 40% of preimplantation embryos formed following normal human sexual reproduction fail to attach to the uterus and are naturally destroyed as a result.

At the blastocyst stage of the preimplantation embryo, no body cells of any type have formed, and even more significantly, there is strong evidence that not even the earliest of events in the chain of events in somatic differentiation have been initiated. A simple way of demonstrating this is by observing subsequent events.

Should the embryo implant in the uterus, the embryo, at approximately 14 days post fertilization will form what is called the primitive streak, this is the first definition that these "seed" cells will form an individual human being as opposed to the forming of two primitive streaks leading to identical twins. Rarely two primitive streaks form that are not completely separated leading to conjoined or Siamese twins. In addition, rarely, two separately fertilized egg cells fuse together to form a single embryo with two different cell types. This natural event leads to a tetragammetic chimera, that is a single human individual with some of the cells in their body being male from the original male embryo, and some cells being female from the original female embryo. These and other simple lessons in embryology teach us that despite the dogmatic assertions of some theologians, the evidence is decisive in support of the position that an individual human life, as opposed to merely cellular life, begins with the primitive streak, (i.e. after 14 days of development). Those who argue that the preimplantation embryo is a person are left with the logical absurdity of ascribing to the blastocyst personhood when we know, scientifically speaking, that no individual exists (i.e. the blastocyst may still form identical twins).

Lifesaving Potential

Human ES cells are nothing other than ICM [inner cell mass] cells grown in the laboratory dish. Because these are pure stem cells uncommitted to any body cell lineage, they may greatly improve the availability of diverse cell types urgently needed in medicine. Human ES cells are unique in that they stand near the base of the developmental tree. These cells are frequently designated "totipotent" stem cells, meaning that they are potentially capable of forming any cell or tissue type needed in medicine. These differ from adult stem cells that are "pluripotent" that is, capable of forming several, but only a limited number, of cell types. An example of pluripotent adult stem cells are the bone marrow stem cells now widely used in the treatment of cancer and other life-threatening diseases.

Some have voiced objection to the use of human ES cells in medicine owing to the source of the cells. Whereas the use of these new technologies has already been carefully debated and approved in the United Kingdom, the United States lags disgracefully behind. I would like to think it is our goodness and our kindness as a people that generates our country's anxieties over these new technologies. Indeed, early in my life I might have argued that since we don't know when a human life begins, it is best not to tamper with the early embryo. That is to say, it is better to be safe than sorry. I believe many U.S. citizens share this initial reaction. But, with time the facts of human embryology and cell biology will be more widely understood. As the Apostle Paul said: "When I was a child, I spake as a child, I understood as a child, I thought as a child: but when I became a man, I put away childish things." (I Cor 13:11) In the same way it is absolutely a matter of life and death that policy makers in the United States carefully study the facts of human embryology and stem cells. A child's understanding of human reproduction simply will not suffice and such ignorance could lead to disastrous consequences.

With appropriate funding of research, we may soon learn to direct these cells to become vehicles of livesaving potential. We may, for instance, become able to produce neurons for the treatment of Parkinson's disease and spinal cord injury, heart muscle cells for heart failure, cartilage for arthritis and many others as well. This research has great potential to help solve the first problem of tissue availability, but the technologies to direct these cells to become various cell types in adequate quantities remains to be elucidated. Because literally hundreds of cell types are needed, thousands of academic research projects need to be funded, far exceeding the resources of the biotechnology industry.

As promising as ES cell technology may seem, it does not solve the remaining problem of histocompatibility [tissue compatibility to allow grafting]. Human ES cells obtained from embryos derived during in vitro fertilization procedures, or from fetal sources, are essentially cells from another individual. . . .

The Problem of Cell Compatibility

An extremely promising solution to this remaining problem of histocompatibility would be to create human ES cells genetically identical to the patient. While no ES cells are known to exist in a developed human being and are therefore not available as a source for therapy, such cells could possibly be obtained through the procedure of somatic cell nuclear transfer (NT), otherwise known as cloning technology. In this procedure, body cells from a patient would be fused with an egg cell that has had its nuclear DNA removed. This would theoretically allow the production of a blastocyst-staged embryo genetically identical to the patient that could, in turn, lead to the production of ES cells identical to the patient. In addition, published data suggests that the procedure of NT can "rejuvenate" an aged cell restoring the proliferative capacity inherent in cells at the beginning of life. This could lead to cellular therapies with an unprecedented opportunity to improve the quality of life for an aging population.

The use of somatic cell nuclear transfer for the purposes of dedifferentiating a patient's cells and obtain autologous undifferentiated stem cells has been designated "Therapeutic Cloning" or alternatively, "Cell Replacement by Nuclear Transfer". This terminology is used to differentiate this clinical indication from the use of NT for the cloning of a child that in turn is designated "Reproductive Cloning". In the United Kingdom, the use of NT for therapeutic cloning has been carefully studied by their Embryology Authority and formally approved by the Parliament.

Ethical Matters

Ethical debates often center over two separate lines of reasoning. Deontological debates are, by nature, focused on our duty to God or our fellow human being. Teleological arguments focus on the question of whether the ends justify the means. Most scholars agree that human ES cell technology and therapeutic cloning offer great pragmatic merit, that is, the teleological arguments in favor of ES and NT technologies are quite strong. The lack of agreement, instead, centers on the deontological arguments relating to the rights of the blastocyst embryo and our duty to protect the individual human life.

I would argue that the lack of consensus is driven by a lack of widespread knowledge of the facts regarding the origins of human life on a cellular level and human life on a somatic and individual level. So the question of when does life begin, is better phrased "when does an individual human life begin." Some dogmatic individuals claim with the same certainty the Church opposed Galileo's claim that the earth is not the center of the universe, that an individual human life begins with the fertilization of the egg cell by the sperm cell. This is superstition, not science. The belief that an individual human being begins with the fertilization of the egg cell by the sperm cell is without basis in scientific fact or, for that matter, without basis in religious tradition.

All strategies to source human cells for the purposes of transplantation have their own unique ethical problems. Because developing embryonic and fetal cells and tissues are "young" and are still in the process of forming mature tissues, there has been considerable interest in obtaining these tissues for use in human medicine. However, the use of aborted embryo or fetal tissue raises numerous issues ranging from concerns over increasing the frequency of elected abortion to simple issues of maintaining quality controls standards in this hypothetical industry. Similarly, obtaining cells and tissues from living donors or cadavers is also not without ethical issues. For instance, an important question is, "Is it morally acceptable to keep 'deceased' individuals on life support for long periods of time in order to harvest organs as they are needed?"

The implementation of ES-based technologies could address some of the ethical problems described above. First, it is important to note that the production of large numbers of human ES cells would not in itself cause these same concerns in accessing human embryonic or fetal tissue, since the resulting cells have the potential to be grown for very long periods of time. Using only a limited number of human embryos not used during in vitro fertilization procedures, could supply many millions of patients if the problem of histocompatibility could be resolved. Second, in the case of NT procedures, the patient may be at lower risk of complications in transplant rejection. Third, the only human cells used would be from the patient. Theoretically, the need to access tissue from other human beings could be reduced.

The Burden Is on Those Who Oppose Stem Cell Research

Having knowledge of a means to dramatically improve the delivery of health care places a heavy burden on the shoulders of those who would actively impede ES and NT technology. The emphasis on the moral error of sin by omission is widely reflected in Western tradition traceable to Biblical tradition. In Matthew chapter 25 we are told of the parable of the master who leaves talents of gold with his servants. One servant, for fear of making a mistake with what was given him, buries the talent in the ground. This servant, labeled "wicked and sloth-ful" in the Bible, reminds us, that simple inaction, when we have been given a valuable asset, is not just a lack of doing good, but is in reality evil. There are times that it is not better to be safe than sorry.

Historically, the United States has a proud history of lead-ing the free world in the bold exploration of new technolo-gies. We did not hesitate to apply our best minds in an effort to allow a man to touch the moon. We were not paralyzed by the fear that like the tower of Babel, we were reaching for the heavens. But a far greater challenge stands before us. We have been given two talents of gold. The first, the human embry-onic stem cell, the second, nuclear transfer technology. Shall we, like the good steward, take these gifts to mankind and courageously use them to the best of our abilities to alleviate the suffering of our fellow human being, or will we fail most miserably and bury these gifts in the earth? This truly is a matter of life and death. I urge you to stand courageously in favor of existing human life. The alternative is to inherit the wind.

"Human beings are not instrumentalities—that is, they are not tools to be used up in the betterment of society."

Embryonic Stem Cell Research Is Unethical

M.D. Harmon

In the following viewpoint, written in June 2004, shortly after the death of former president Ronald Reagan from Alzheimer's disease, M.D. Harmon criticizes the idea that a suitable tribute to Reagan would be lifting the ban on federal funding for embryonic stem cell research on new stem lines. Embryonic stem-cell research involves using stem cells from early stage human embryos to repair or replace damaged cells in patients suffering from diseases such as Alzheimer's. Removing the stem cells, however, destroys the embryo. Harmon believes that embryonic cells are human beings that deserve the protection afforded to adult humans and that destroying them is unethical. Harmon is an editorial writer for the Portland Press Herald *in Portland, Maine.*

As you read, consider the following questions:

1. What does Harmon believe humanity should have learned from twentieth-century history?

2. What scientific argument does the author offer against using embryonic stem cells?

M.D. Harmon, "Is Push for Embryonic Stem Cell Research Worthy of a Reagan?" *Portland Press Herald,* June 14, 2004. Copyright © 2004 by Blethen Maine Newspapers, Inc. Reproduced by permission of *Portland Press Herald/Maine Sunday Telegram.* Reproduction does not imply endorsement.

3. Why does Harmon criticize those linking Ronald Reagan with support for embryonic stem cell research?

After a week's worth of eulogies (and a few "dislogies") about Ronald Reagan, there's precious little I can add.

Except to say that many of my columns have been, in one sense or another, inspired at least in part by his trust in God and his belief in his country. There is, however, one thread in some comments about Reagan that is worth addressing: the idea that the former president, who suffered greatly from Alzheimer's disease, would be suitably memorialized if President [George W.] Bush would change his policy strictly limiting the use of embryonic stem cells for medical research.

The commentators typically refer to Nancy Reagan's support for the idea, but they skip over inconvenient facts—and a similarly inconvenient moral point.

If you want the testimony of another first lady with credibility on this issue, there's Laura Bush, who refused [in June 2004] to endorse embryonic stem cell research even though her father died of Alzheimer's. "We have to be really careful between what we want to do for science and what we should do ethically," she said.

Lessons of the Twentieth Century

Speaking of ethics, didn't the history of the 20th century teach us that human beings are not instrumentalities—that is, they are not tools to be used up in the betterment of society? Did we not learn that such a view is the totalitarian view of humanity, not the one that respects human rights?

But, we are told, there are so many embryos—fertilized eggs, genetically completely human, containing all the DNA that you or I have—sitting around in freezers as the result of in vitro fertility treatments. Won't they just be "wasted" if we don't use them for experimentation?

Well, I remember a time when "wasted" meant "killed," and that's the impact of slicing and dicing these tiny human beings for research. Do we really lack the moral imagination that otherwise lets us see that each one of us now walking around was once exactly as they are?

If we produce "excess" embryos, perhaps the place to start the questioning is in the rationale for their production, rather than in wondering how to use them up for our benefit.

Advocates say they are valuable because they can morph into any body cell, and thus perhaps replace cells lost by disease, including Reagan's Alzheimer's.

Trouble is, that's not what the scientists are saying. Robert Lanza, medical director of the company Advanced Cell Technology, wrote in the May 24 [2004] *Scientific American* that adult tissue routinely rejects embryonic cells, and it would take "millions of discarded embryos" to create stem-cell lines useful for research.

Lanza favors cloning, which would theoretically create tissue identical to the donor's that would not suffer rejection, but Americans are rightly queasy about duplicating people.

Two more things always seem to be left out of the advocates' talking points on this issue.

The Adult Stem Cell Alternative

The first is that there are adult stem cells that share many, if not all, of the adaptive characteristics of embryonic cells.

While embryonic experimentation has stalled, research on adult cells, taken without killing the donor, has produced remarkable early results in addressing sickle-cell anemia, juvenile diabetes and other diseases.

Indeed, tying embryonic cells to a cure for Alzheimer's appears to be either a tactic of ignorance or a deliberately deceptive campaign. As Rick Weiss, a *Washington Post* reporter, noted in an article [in June 2004], "Of all the diseases that may someday be cured by embryonic stem cell treatments, Alzheimer's is the least likely to benefit."

Breen. © 2001 by Copley News Service. Reproduced by permission.

Or, as researcher Ronald D.G. McKay of the National Institute of Neurological Disorders and Stroke put it in Weiss' article, "To start with, people need a fairy tale. Maybe that's unfair, but they tell a story line that's relatively easy to understand."

Whether it's true or not apparently just isn't all that important.

Ronald Reagan's Pro-Life Legacy

There is a second point, and it is also telling: It is virtually impossible that Reagan, one of the most staunchly pro-life presidents in our history, would have consented to his wife's campaign.

The proof is not only contained in his many speeches on the topic, but in a slim pro-life book he wrote in 1983 called *Abortion and the Conscience of the Nation*. These words it contains are also part of his legacy:

"Every legislator, every doctor, and every citizen needs to recognize that the real issue is whether to affirm and protect the sanctity of all human life, or to embrace a social ethic where some human lives are valued and others are not.

"As a nation, we must choose between the sanctity of life ethic and the 'quality of life' ethic. I have no trouble identifying the answer our nation has always given to this basic question, and the answer that I hope and pray it will give in the future."

Seeking to dissect tiny humans in Reagan's name is a sad and unworthy way to attempt to pay tribute to this great man.

> *"Equating compassion with forced death is part of a dramatic reorientation of social thought on human rights, personhood and the role of law insofar as it impacts the meaning of human dignity."*

Euthanasia Is Unethical

Edward J. Richard

Edward J. Richard is an attorney and a Roman Catholic priest. He teaches moral theology at Kenrick-Glennon Seminary in St. Louis, Missouri, and is a member of the board of directors at the Center for Bioethics and Culture. In the following viewpoint Richard argues against euthanasia, asserting that innocent human beings should not be killed by any act or omission, even if to relieve suffering. Using the controversy surrounding the case of Terri Schiavo, the Florida woman whose life support was finally discontinued after her family battled for years over her medical treatment, Richard argues that severely disabled people deserve respect and legal protection. He believes that their deaths should not be hastened by denying them care.

As you read, consider the following questions:

1. How does Richard relate human death to the preservation of human life?

2. Why does the author disapprove of the term "vegeta-tive" to describe human beings?

3. According to Richard, in what way did medicine and law fail Terri Schiavo?

At Easter, Christians recall the singular event of the bodily resurrection of the person of Jesus Christ. The event was a decisive victory over the greatest threat to the human sense of dignity, death itself.

The heartbreak of each human death, however, continues to illustrate in part why the preservation of physical human life is necessary and why the death of an innocent human being should not be directly caused by any action or omission, even if to relieve suffering.

The tragic saga of Terri Schiavo—allegedly in a persistent vegetative state—marks the current level of confusion arising from a loss of the sense of the meaning of the human person, a unity of body and soul, the basis of many age-old laws relating to social order, including the prohibition against euthanasia.

Two Views of End of Life Issues

Terri's story gained national attention because many concerned people believe that dying with dignity does not mean that Terri should die due to a court-ordered insult to her person through deprivation of food and water. For these, many Christians among them, Terri is a living, breathing human person whose life is of unimaginable value and is worthy of protection and basic care.

On the other hand, for many people who support the withdrawal of Terri's food and water, some Christians included, dying that way is a matter of right. In the words of her husband's lawyer, George Felos, "Just because Terri Schiavo is not conscious doesn't mean she doesn't have dignity." Thus the right to die becomes, for the rest of society, a duty, something we must accept and provide for her.

On another level, it is argued, compassionate people would go along with withdrawing her food and water. This view, equating compassion with forced death, is part of a dramatic reorientation of social thought on human rights, personhood and the role of law insofar as it impacts the meaning of human dignity.

Those who accept euthanasia, assisted suicide, or withdrawal of feeding and hydration from severely disabled persons believe that terminating a life to end its burden is just and reasonable. They can, in a way, point to the freedom from the burdensome life now lived. Death by design, rather than care, becomes a justifiable means of relieving the burden of such a life. In cases like Terri's, her legally protected freedom and dignity now seems to require her death. "Death with dignity" has long been the catchphrase of the euthanasia movement.

The Limits of Medicine

The troubling thing with the slogan "death with dignity" is that it has no clear meaning or limits. Quite rightly, no one should have to accept becoming a victim of therapeutic tyranny or overzealous treatment beyond reason. Terri's alleged condition, the so-called persistent vegetative state, is one most people know very little about. Even for the expert, it is only a hypothesis. Most people do not realize that misdiagnosis and varying degrees of recovery are common to this category of medical cases. One study reported that 40 percent of these cases are misdiagnosed. In Terri's case, there is wide disagreement among the experts. But, all agree, Terri is alive.

Moreover, the term "vegetative" applied to any living woman offends human dignity. Living human beings are never forms of plant life. In practice, the vegetative description has become a self-fulfilling prophecy for the victims, since very little attention is given to adequate means of diagnosis, treatment and rehabilitation of these persons in the United States.

Comment from an Aggrieved Family

[Our] family would encourage the media to remember that [the Terri Schiavo] case was allegedly about "Terri's choice." There is absolutely no evidence that Terri wanted to die of dehydration, or that she believed that the level of one's disability gives anyone the moral and legal right to end another's life. . . .

[The independent medical examiner] said clearly that dehydration, not her brain injury, was the cause of her death. Terri was dehydrated to death before our eyes. The moral shame of what happened is not erased because of Terri's level of disability. No one would say that "blind people" or "brain-injured" people should be put to death. That would be an irresponsible and heartless position to take. Tragically, that is what happened to Terri. As a society, it seems that we have lost our compassion for the disabled.

Schindler Family Statement on Medical Examiner's Report,
http://www.terrisfight.org/statement.html, June 16, 2005.

It is far more common for them to be abandoned to death than it is for attempts to be made to help the patient improve with even simple therapies. The excuse for this is always the same: We cannot guarantee recovery.

Even if Terri would not wish to continue indefinitely with medical treatment, we are not justified in concluding that withdrawing basic care such as food and water is compassionate or dignified.

Many people die from disease because no treatment exists to stop the progression of the disease toward inevitable death. Terri's condition is similar to those only insofar as the competence of current medical practice is surpassed by the enormous challenge of the affliction. Unlike cases such as terminal cancer, Terri is not dying. Nothing about Terri's condition makes her "terminal." In this case, Terri will die because she will not receive food and water in the way that is appropriate for her condition.

The Limits of the Law

Terri and others like her are at risk because they have disabilities that are not terminal but are difficult for the current state of medicine and because they have insufficient legal protection. The law has abandoned doctrines which afford protection to human beings in significant cases where life is most vulnerable.

The use of words and phrases in the law like nonviable, permanently unconscious and vegetative tell part of the story. Even common language takes sides in these cases. Increasingly, with the shrouding of the human realities such terms imply, the law makes no effort to critically assess the role of some dangerous limitations that contribute to the deadly outcome of these cases, like the limits of medicine's ability to prognosticate and treat.

In Terri's case, a number of Americans have seen what law and medicine could not. Terri's humanity and its dignity mean that she should be guaranteed basic care including food and water. It is now time to begin asking how medicine and law can legitimately serve to bolster respect for and improve the lives of persons with disabilities like Terri's, not sanction their deaths. Unfortunately for Terri, needed improvements in the law will probably be too late.[1]

---

1. In fact, food and water were withdrawn, and Schiavo died.

"I affirm that the choice of death with dignity . . . is a moral and a more godly choice than passively enduring a life pointlessly devoid of hope or meaning."

Euthanasia Is Ethical

John Shelby Spong

John Shelby Spong is a theologian and the retired bishop of the Episcopal diocese of Newark, New Jersey. His books include Why Christianity Must Change or Die *and* A New Christianity for a New World: Why Traditional Faith Is Dying and How a New Faith Is Being Born. *In the following viewpoint Spong argues that because modern medical advancements now prolong the death process, human beings have a moral responsibility to participate in their own end-of-life decisions. Spong urges Christians to find meaning and holiness in death and to participate with God in choosing to end life when it is radically compromised by illness or injury.*

As you read, consider the following questions:

1. How did Paul and other early Christians define death, according to Spong?

2. How does the author describe the positive impact of death on human lives?

3. Why does Spong reject the "slippery slope" argument that legalizing assisted suicide will lead to coercive

pressure on elderly patients to end their lives prematurely?

A century ago it was not an option. The final moments of life came with no heart pump or ventilators, no shrinking of tumors with radiation, no ability to cleanse a person's blood supply. Death was normally quick, since medical science had little help to offer. Then came the quantum leap in medical knowledge that expanded longevity beyond anyone's fondest dreams.

I rejoice in these incredible human accomplishments, grieving only at their limited availability across the world. Religious leaders universally applaud these medical advances that seem to validate the claim that life is sacred and calls us anew to acknowledge and even to worship the Source of this sacred life, whose name, they proclaim, is God.

These stunning developments, however, did not come without raising huge issues. If death is not as inescapable as it once was, a whole new level of decision making must be engaged. We are no longer simply children leaning on the Deity with no responsibility except to embrace our destiny. New dimensions of maturity become obvious. We now share in the life and death decisions that once were thought to lie solely in the domain of God.

There is no virtue in refusing to accept this new human reality. Nothing is changed by hiding our heads in the sand. This revolution has called us to frontiers where many religious ideas about the end of life must be set aside as no longer fitting our world. When that occurs, assisted suicide—under certain conditions—emerges as a new alternative for Christian people; the values marking the Christian faith and those motivating the 'Death with Dignity' movement begin to merge. The key to this union lies in the commitment by both groups to defend the dignity and sacredness of human life. That is a rapprochement I welcome and hope to facilitate.

When Does a Person Have a Duty to Die?

1. A duty to die is more likely when continuing to live will impose significant burdens—emotional burdens, extensive caregiving, destruction of life plans, and, yes, financial hardship—on your family and loved ones. This is the fundamental insight underlying a duty to die.

2. A duty to die becomes greater as you grow older. As we age, we will be giving up less by giving up our lives, if only because we will sacrifice fewer remaining years of life and a smaller portion of our life plans. After all, it's not as if we would be immortal and live forever if we could just manage to avoid a duty to die. To have reached the age of, say, seventy-five or eighty years without being ready to die is itself a moral failing, the sign of a life out of touch with life's basic realities.

3. A duty to die is more likely when you have already lived a full and rich life. You have already had a full share of the good things life offers.

4. There is greater duty to die if your loved ones' lives have already been difficult or impoverished, if they have had only a small share of the good things that life has to offer (especially if through no fault of their own). . . .

John Hardwig, "Is There a Duty to Die?"
Hastings Center Report, 1997.

Redefining the Christian Concept of Death

As these new realities engage both groups, core definitions demand to be recast. For Christians that will not be easy. Just as we have come to believe that St. Paul was wrong in his attitude toward women and homosexuality, we now must see that he was also wrong when he viewed death as an enemy, even the "the last enemy" that had to be destroyed. When Paul wrote those words, he was under the influence of the ancient biblical myth of creation.

In that story, first thought of quite literally and later regarded as only metaphorically true, the explanation was offered that the disobedience of the first man and woman had plunged the whole world into sin, breaking the divine image in human life and causing banishment from the Garden of Eden. This fall was also said to have destroyed our immortality, causing us ultimately to die. The fact that no one escaped death was *prima facie* evidence for those like Paul, who were shaped by this defining myth, that sin was universal and death, its punishment, was the ultimate human enemy that had to be overcome.

It is easy to understand how ancient people came to these conclusions, since death was a lurking presence ready to pounce upon its victims at every stage of life. This biblical definition of death, however, is clearly wrong and must be dismissed as no longer operative. It is not even a correct metaphor.

Death is not divine punishment endured because we are fallen people. Death is a natural part of life's cycle. It must, therefore, be embraced as something good—a friend, not an enemy. Can any of us really imagine life without death being a part of it? Far from being evil, death is simply that shadow which gives life its passion, its depth, its sense of urgency. Death walks with us from the moment we are born. It pressures life. It is that reality which makes life's experiences unrepeatable. Childhood lasts but a limited time. It should be neither rushed nor restrained. The same is true for our adolescence, adulthood, and every other identifiable stage of our lives. There is only one journey through the middle years, the aging process, and into old age itself. Each stage must be grasped with vigor.

How Modern Medicine Has Changed Death

Life is meant to be lived. We are to scale its heights, plumb its depths, and taste its sweetness. Death rings the bell on all procrastination. It cannot, therefore, be our enemy, something we strive to defeat. It is our friend, something we must learn to accept as an ultimate source of life's meaning. When modern medicine pushes death back in order to expand the length and quality of our existence, it is not defeating our enemy, it is revealing our holiness.

But a perilous boundary becomes visible in this new consciousness when the efforts of medical science cease expanding the length and quality of life, and begin postponing death's inevitability. When that subtle and poorly defined moment comes, a new arena is entered where both a new Christian belief system and a new ethic about final things needs to be born.

Do we honor the God of life by extending the length of our days when the quality of our life has dissipated? Is a breathing cadaver a witness to the God of life? Should powerful narcotics be used to lessen our pain and thus to extend our days even if they rob us of the relationships which give life its meaning?

If I have a medically-confirmed incurable disease, and can bear the pain of that sickness only by being placed into a kind of twilight zone, where I neither recognize the sweet smile of my wife nor respond to the touch of her hand, do I not have the ethical right to end my life with medical assistance? Can dedicated Christians step into this process and say we have now reached the point in human development where we have not just the right, but the moral obligation, to share life-and-death decisions with God? Do we not serve our deepest convictions if we decide to end our life at the moment in which its sacredness becomes compromised?

I am one Christian who wants to say not just one 'yes' to these questions, but Yes! Yes! A thousand times yes! I want to do it not in the guilt of yesterday's value system that proclaimed that only God could properly make these decisions. I want to do it, rather, as a modern Christian, asserting that human skill has brought about a new maturity in which we are both called to and equipped for the awesome task of being co-creators with God of the gift of life. As such we must also be responsible with God for guaranteeing the goodness of our deaths.

What About the "Slippery Slope?"

I am not put off by the slippery slope arguments that are so often used by religious forces and that resort to fearmongering when they cannot embrace the new realities. I do not believe that this stance will lead to state-ordered executions of the elderly, or to health maintenance organizations curtailing medical payments until a quick death is achieved. I do not believe that greedy potential heirs will use this power to hasten the receipt of their inheritances. These are, in my mind, nothing but the smokescreens of negativity, designed to play on the fear present when childlike dependency is threatened and when mature human decisions are mandated.

A world that is bright enough to create these opportunities is surely bright enough to control those who might misuse them. All of these abuses could be eliminated by investing this life-and-death decision solely with the affected individual. Advance directives, signed when that person is in good health, should be honored. The decision-making power should reside with the individual, who alone is to be granted the legal right to determine how and when his or her life is to come to an end. That is how we will surround death with the dignity that this ancient friend deserves. I regard this choice as a right to be enshrined alongside "life, liberty, and the pursuit of happiness" at the center of our value system, a basic human freedom that we must claim.

Above all, I affirm that the choice of death with dignity, whether by my own hand or with the assistance of my physician, is a moral and a more godly choice than passively enduring a life pointlessly devoid of hope or meaning. I believe this option is rooted in the Christian conviction that life is sacred. It is thus not life denying, but life affirming. It is because we honor life that we want to end it with our faculties still intact, our minds still competent, and our dignity still respected. Assisted suicide, as a conscious choice made amid the extremity of sickness, is the way that I, as a Christian, can pay homage to the Christ who stands at the center of that faith, whose purpose, says the Fourth Gospel, was to bring life and to bring it abundantly.

To accept the responsibility of making ultimate decisions about life; to celebrate the fact that I live in an age of remarkable ingenuity; to embrace the truth that death is not our enemy but the shadow that gives life its purpose; to claim the right to determine how and when I shall die; these are the opportunities that confront people in the 21st century. I embrace them as a Christian who deeply believes in the God who is the Source of Life, who makes all life holy.

I shall live as deeply as I can while I have the opportunity. I hope to end my life as gracefully as circumstances will allow. But in both my living and my dying, even if that dying is by my own choice or hand in the face of the end of meaning and dignity, I want to assert that my decisions are within the framework of what I call Christian ethics.

> *"[Through cloning, the] biblical view of man as a special creation in the image of God will be deconstructed, and the idea that we are no more than our genes will take life."*

Cloning Is Immoral

Brian Caulfield

In the following viewpoint Brian Caulfield calls cloning immoral. According to Caulfield, cloning deconstructs the Christian notion of a human being as a special creation made in the image of God. He argues that reproductive cloning devalues life and distorts the meaning of existence. Caulfield links reproductive cloning to abortion and to a broader "culture of death" that denies the unique value of each human life. Caulfield is a Catholic journalist who writes for the weekly archdiocesan newspaper Catholic New York.

As you read, consider the following questions:

1. What does Caulfield identify as the "bad news" about reproductive cloning?
2. What are some examples of the "culture of death," cited by the author?
3. According to Caulfield, what concepts from the philosophy of John Paul II have especially influenced his thinking?

My son was born last fall [2000] in the way of Caesar [i.e., by Cesarian section], seven weeks before he was due. It truly was a blessed event, which is to say it was in no way easy. I held my wife's hand in the operating room, whispering the Rosary in her ear and watching for the faint nod of her head each time I said the name "Jesus," knowing then that she was still all right.

My wife and child rode the tide between life and death, as a dozen professionals with the world's most sophisticated instruments coaxed them toward the shore.

"She's losing too much blood."

"The cord is wrapped twice around his neck."

I was at the head of the operating table, shielded from the action by a drape, left to imagine the worst. I heard a baby cry, louder each time and less breathless. A smile was on the pale lips of my wife and her tired eyes were beaming, and I realized, rather dumbly, that it was my child crying. This was our son. A nurse from the other side of the drape, which had seemed a world away, called out, "Does the father want to see the baby?"

"Yes!" I cried before I knew I had spoken. He was crinkly, pink, and no longer crying as she held his tiny body in that trained and tender way nurses have. I saw then that medicine still operates much as it always has amid the wonderful machinery: It's still about blood and humors and the human touch. It's about a mystery which the fine line of an EKG [electrocardiogram] can only point to.

Modern Reproductive and Scientific Developments

Science seeks to enter more deeply into this mystery. Dread diseases have been virtually eliminated, organs are transplanted or mechanically made, and the very building blocks of life in the human genome are being decoded.

Yet new dangers are also confronting us. There's the chemical abortion pill, RU-486, which Planned Parenthood here in New York is marketing to teenagers in subway ads as the "early option pill." There's the "emergency contraception" regimen, which actually causes an early abortion by making the uterine wall hostile to the implantation of a newly fertilized ovum. Fighting these lethal methods politically, legally, and in the court of public opinion takes immense effort and funding. Yet abortion is just the tip of the iceberg.

Stem-cell research on aborted babies will go on in private labs, whether there is federal funding or not, and genetic engineering could well bring us to a Brave New World of designer humans. And what of the thousands of frozen embryos in suspended animation in labs throughout the world? Numbers of pro-life women have come forward to offer their bodies as hosts to these little ones, an Operation Rescue of another sort.

Others regretfully hold that the frozen lives must be allowed to expire "naturally," as they do after 10 or so years. These pro-lifers say the only way to make good of a bad situation is to allow the embryos to expire in the frozen state, letting God and nature take their course.

These are the roads technology has thrust us along, leaving no easy way back to firm moral footing. I worry not so much for myself as for my son, who has given me a stake in the next generation. I look at him sleeping, his arms spread wide in cruciform as though to embrace what will come, and wonder what world he will inherit. Every father throughout history has wondered the same about his child, but what I ponder is not what the world will be like with the coming of the next mechanical marvel—the successor to the automobile, the airplane, the Internet. These are advances in the external world, the shaping and remaking of the stuff of creation. What my son faces is more personal and internal, a scientific manipulation of the building blocks not only of matter but of man—that enfleshed, spiritual mystery of a being.

I imagine that God will step in and say "enough" before the first human clone, refusing to infuse a soul into the Petri-dish being. He may call the final curtain down on us all for letting this go on, or He may confuse us as at Babel for seeking to speak His language. Yet some scientists say it is just a matter of time. Most of us don't even know what the word "clone" means. It conjures up images of identical twins (triplets? quadruplets?) "hard-wired" in their genes to walk, talk, and think alike, the stuff of science fiction.

Cloning Devalues Life

But the facts make for a much grimmer scenario. The attempt to clone means the destruction of thousands of human lives conceived artificially for the purpose of experimentation. Every part of that sentence is bad news. First, the very attempt to clone means treating human life in general, and the human life under experimentation in particular, as a means and not as an end in itself. The whole notion of unrepeatable individuality and bodily integrity—of life, liberty, and the pursuit of happiness—upon which so much of our social, legal, and emotional life is based will be threatened. The biblical view of man as a special creation in the image of God will be deconstructed, and the idea that we are no more than our genes will take life. The soul will grow cold, as fewer and fewer believe that man even has one.

Technically speaking, embryonic lives will be brought into being in dishes only to have the genetic information of their nuclei removed and replaced with the genetic information from the cells of another human being, the "donor." The newly concocted embryo will then be implanted in the womb of a woman, a "host mother," to grow in the normal way for nine months and be born into the world as a genetic copy of the "donor."

They say it has been done with the sheep Dolly and other animals after hundreds of failed attempts. Man is a more sophisticated organism, scientists say, so thousands more embryos may have to be made and discarded before the experiment "takes" and a thriving, dividing life is implanted in a "host."

What are the reasons for engaging in such genetic monkey business? Humanitarian; of course, we are told by scientists and ethicists. Better health, longer lives. But whose health and lives are we talking about? One can imagine a genetic match for Mom—call her Mom minor—providing skin, organs, maybe even brain cells as Mom starts forgetting where she put her glasses. Better yet, who knows if she'll even need glasses after "nonessential" elements of Mom minor's eyes have been transplanted? And how about when Mom minor reaches her majority? Could the two not have a long and loving relationship, donating genes and cells and making another replica to add to their genetic family? The possibilities are endless. Or will they end us?

Reproductive Cloning Is Not Reincarnation

A glimpse into the modern moral mind was given in a February [2001] cover story on cloning in the *New York Times Magazine*. Featured was a space-suit-clad man from France named Rael, who among other projects has raised $7 million for a center to welcome aliens in style. He and his odd followers, called Raelians, have labs working overtime to produce the first human clone. They claim to have the genetic material of a dead child and the financial backing of the child's grieving parents, who want to bring him back to life, so to speak. The *Times* writer takes a rather dim view of the Raelians (though some, she reports, are legitimate scientists with prestigious day jobs). But the subtle moral censure in the story centers not so much on cloning itself or the destruction of many tiny lives in the process. The problem with the Raelians' project, the article says, is that it raises false hopes for grieving parents. After all, a genetically identical child is not really the same child. Cloning is a genetic replication, not a resurrection or reincarnation. You can never reproduce the circumstances, influences, and experiences that make up the reality of each person. The people involved seem to know this yet not know it, the author observes. By the end of the article, the Raelians come off as somewhat idealistic zealots who are cruel and deluded in a clinical sort of way.

Though the author may not intend it—she cites favorably some scientists who oppose cloning—her lack of a cohesive moral view beyond "informed choice" sends an invitation to cloners and their apologists: If you're going to do this, you'd better find deeper reasons than restoring a dead child to his parents.

The fact that the usually cool heads at the *Times* are having trouble mixing cloning in their ethical palette is evident from the magazine's cover illustration. In the style of a sensational science-fiction comic book, it shows two identical babies and screaming headlines: "Lab of the Human Clones!" "Rich U.F.O. Sect Behind Scheme." The sci-fi treatment is needed because the serious, considered arguments from respected experts that the *Times* trots out to support abortion and all its technological offspring are not yet on the same page. Even the Dolly clone-master says that human experiments would be irresponsible, given the number of embryos that would have to be destroyed. The *Times* seems in a way to be preparing the field, clearing out the wacky Rael scientists who give cloning a bad name so as to leave room for the "real" scientists who work not for the base reasons of meeting the emotional needs of distraught parents, but for the advancement of knowledge and the betterment of humanity. Expect the *Times*, when the time is ripe, to replace the nucleus of its own coverage, from comic-book colors to white-coated, serious-looking scientists.

Reproductive Cloning and the Mystery of Existence

What can be done will be done, some say must be done, in the name of "science." Yet the questions of man and his meaning—the mystery of existence—remain. The mystery is more evident to me than ever as I hold my son, Stephen James, now six months old. He has my mouth, cheeks, and chin and my fair skin. He has my wife's nose and her brown eyes. She puts him in the crib beside our bed after I have kissed him goodnight, and she says that we sleep in the same position, with the same facial expression, and both of us have the habit of grinding our teeth and talking in our sleep.

He is a mix of our genes, yet is very much himself. He lives by the touches and smiles, words and hugs of his parents. Yet on the rare occasions we let him out of our sight for more than a minute, we return to find him sucking his thumb or staring at a shadow on the wall. He needs us for his very life of food, warmth, and hygiene, yet he exists apart from us, with interests, attitudes and a schedule of sleeping and eating which we can influence but not fully change. At his tender age, Stephen James is his own man, with some inner motive directing him. Holding him once I thought, in a flash of intuition about abortion: "What God has joined, let no man put asunder." I was thinking nothing new. Marriage and the good of children are intrinsically, spiritually, and physically linked. Let one be broken at will, the other will be vulnerable to destruction or manipulation.

I cradle my little boy's precious head, so fragile and so perfectly formed. How could anyone do it? To crush a skull such as this in abortion requires the coolly calculating mind of a serial killer. For a nation to allow it to go on at the count of thousands per day requires a blindness of immense proportions. To promote it in politics and defend it in courts would take the soul of a people away.

Why Reproductive Cloning Should Be Banned

Beyond [the] considerations inherent to cloning itself, there are a number of practical concerns. Cloning is the opening wedge for a series of new technologies that will ultimately lead to designer babies and one that is likely to become feasible much sooner than genetic engineering. If we get used to cloning in the near term, it will be much harder to oppose germ-line engineering for enhancement purposes in the future. It is important to lay down a political marker at an early point to demonstrate that the development of these technologies is not inevitable, and that societies can take some measure of control over the pace and scope of technological advance. There is no strong constituency in favor of cloning in any country. It is also an area where considerable international consensus exists in opposition to the procedure. Cloning therefore represents an important strategic opportunity to establish the possibility of political control over biotechnology.

Francis Fukuyama, Our Posthuman Future: Consequences of the Biotechnology Revolution, *2002.*

As a new father, thrust into the world of life insurance, tax deductions, infant health coverage and the Universal Gifts to Minors Act, my thoughts occasionally stray to the weightier question already posed: What world will Stephen James inherit? I say "inherit" because I do not see the future as something we choose to give the next generation. By the time we are ready to leave the world to them, our children usually are very much in the thick of things. They are heirs, not recipients of favor, and this status begins from the time of conception, as even the civil law of inheritance at times allows. Their right to inherit is inherent.

We can lose sight of this in a culture that speaks of every child "wanted" and children of "choice." That parents can write their offspring out of their wills, and treat pets and charitable foundations as if they were blood relations, is indicative of broken connections in society. Today, it is another manifestation of the Culture of Death that a father can treat his son as though he didn't exist, as though their natural relationship made no inescapable demands. Somehow it is of a piece with "no-fault" divorce, male-abandoned households, and abortion. Natural, biological bonds no longer bind. Life is not in the blood. "Love" is not, as true love is, an act of the will drawn forth by the value of the other person and the nature of the relationship, but merely a preference, a pleasure, an arrangement of compatibility and convenience.

When I'm awakened by infant cries at 4:30 for the fourth straight morning, my emotions and foggy consciousness tell me that this is unfair and I have every right to roll over. Yet a love that is far from a warm, fuzzy feeling moves my body to the kitchen to heat the formula as my wife, who had the midnight shift, sleeps. It is no longer I who live, but my son living in me. He is my heir, therefore he is my love, even at 4:30 on a winter morning. I work for us; the future is ours. About the third time I held him, while he was still hooked up to beeping machines in the neonatal intensive care unit, I realized that there would never be a moment for the rest of my life when I would not be aware of his existence.

Reproductive Cloning and the Theology of John Paul II

I had lived much of my life with the convenient notion that nothing of this world could hold me close. I could walk away from any situation and person—even ones that could benefit me—if they did not suit my form of morals. It was a quasi-spiritualism that passed for Catholicism, until I learned about the social teachings of the Church and the personalism of

Pope John Paul II. Before we make a single conscious choice, we are in necessary and binding relationships by virtue of biological and psychological facts, the body and the soul. A child conceived through fornication bears no sin for that act; yet he must find and define himself in the context of the illicit relationship. The same for a test-tube child, or a cloned one. Whatever our circumstances, we must grapple with the structures of objective reality.

A libertarian friend of mine was telling me of the ideal society, in which all legal and social relations would be freely chosen and no obligations would obtain except to refrain from doing physical harm. It sounded awful to me, and I asked if a mother would be obligated to care for her newborn. My friend, looking beyond his logic, admitted that maybe this one exception would need to be made. I suggested that his exception is really the rule. Does not how we are carried in the womb of one woman and born helpless into the world tell us something about the human condition? Are we ever so independent of others that the law should see us as solipsists? Whatever choices we make, there will always be human proportions—relationships, friendships, and the inner landscape of "I"

There is no escape from the personal: This is the point I get from the Pope. No way to transcend or computerize the conditions and the responsive obligations of the "I-Thou," the "Self and Other." We cannot choose when and how to be human. We cannot choose whether to be a part of the unfolding drama of man, to be our father's son or our brother's keeper. We already are. We are free to choose, and the greatest freedom is the truth. What can be done must not be done when it is false. The project of man is not so much to do more as to be more: more authentic, more faithful, more loving.

Immanuel Kant's categorical imperative, which has led the modern mind to inhuman conclusions, must give way to the interpersonal imperative. By placing the source of all knowledge and value within the mind, Kant opened a door to a lethal relativism. He said that we should act only in accordance with what we see as a universal moral law. But what if my particular reading of this law includes the killing of Jews or "my body, my choice?" You have your truth, I have mine.

Yet there is a Voice and a Way beyond the structures of the self. I hear this when the Pope says, "Be not afraid! Do not fear man!" We are in the image of God; we share a paternity, we are a family. We do not simply define others and ourselves in the confines of the mind but discover them in the wonders of the world. We should accept the "I-Thou," the relationship of Self to Other which we enter not by choice but by birth. We should surrender to it, without forsaking the necessary "I" which is my stake in the relationship. It is a way of losing your life to find it again; the very heart of the Gospel. It is what gets me up at 4:30 a.m. on a winter weekday.

> *"Cloning and other advanced medical technologies, no matter how much they shake up our worldviews, are essentially on the side of life."*

Cloning Is Moral

Gregory Stock

The author of Redesigning Humans: Our Inevitable Genetic Future, *Gregory Stock is the director of the Program on Medicine, Technology, and Society at the University of California School of Public Health in Los Angeles. In the following viewpoint Stock argues that cloning, since it perpetuates life, is not immoral. Moreover, according to Stock, humans have an ethical obligation to pursue biomedical research that promises to improve human life. He contends that when reproductive cloning of humans succeeds it will not lead to the horrors imagined by opponents. Identical twins, he points out, are clones, and nobody objects to them.*

As you read, consider the following questions:

1. What is Stock's view of the relationship between religion and science?
2. In Stock's opinion, why can't embryos be considered human?
3. Why does the author believe that U.S. scientists should take a leading role in cloning research?

Last Sunday's [November 25, 2001,] report of the first cloning of a human embryo had pundits wringing their hands. The announcement by a small biotech firm in Massachusetts, however, was pure hype. The researchers had not even formed viable human embryos—just fertilized eggs with their nuclei replaced that divided a few times, then died. Korean researchers reported the same thing a few years ago. Such experiments are a long way from human cloning, since a few cellular divisions can occur even in the absence of viable chromosomes.

But the reports couldn't have come at a better time for Congress, which is eager to regulate this arena and is planning to take action early [in 2002]. We have to hope that this time out they come up with something very different from the Weldon bill, a draconian measure passed by the house [in July 2001] that would have made scientists using cloning techniques in their quest for treatments for Parkinson's, diabetes, and other diseases subject to 10 years in prison. The bill also would have criminalized the importation of the products of such research, so if progress were made in Britain, where such research is legal, and Americans went there for treatment, they could be jailed upon their return for bringing home the cells in their flesh.[1]

It is frightening that an arcane theological debate about whether or not a tiny speck of cells is a human being could force a promising field of basic biomedical research to flee the United States for foreign countries. A consensus will never exist about moral questions of this sort. Even in the religious community, opinions differ. In Judaism and Islam, personhood begins about a month after conception, and before a proclamation by Pope Pius IX in 1869, even in Catholicism, ensoulment occurred not at conception, but after several weeks.

1. Despite several attempts at drafting federal regulations on cloning research, none had been signed into law as of November 2005.

Religion vs. Science

Religion has an important place in our hearts and lives, but it should not shape science policy. If Catholic dogma were our guide, birth control pills would be illegal; children of in-vitro fertilization would not exist, and evolution would only recently have been taught in school.

To oppose therapeutic cloning or its funding is one thing, to criminalize it quite another. It is beyond me how a majority of our Congressional representatives could argue for this when it is legal for a woman to have an abortion or to discard an embryo for any reason whatsoever. Do they see no inconsistency in guarding the right to destroy a 3-month-old fetus, while putting a doctor in jail for an experiment on a microscopic dot of cells that could legally be flushed down a toilet?

To imbue a few cells in a Petri dish with human rights defies common sense. They lack a fundamental necessity for coming forth into our world—a connection to a warm, nurturing womb. Elevating their protection above the needs of medical research that might save millions of real people suffering from real diseases shows a profound disregard for human life.

Some argue that blocking this research will stop cloning. But they are deluding themselves. Over 300 animals have been cloned, some 200 have survived, and most are healthy. Cloning a human is too dangerous at present, but wait a few years. We will see a human clone within the decade. And it won't destroy our values any more than a "test tube" baby did. Do people's brains go dead when they hear the word *clone* ? I've seen otherwise sane individuals respond with diatribes about growing people to harvest their organs. But chopping an organ out of a clone would be just as much a murder as killing any other person. Clones are merely delayed identical twins. The idea is a bit strange, but clones are just not that threatening. You may already know one. Identical twins are clones, and though they're similar, they're unique individuals.

The Dignity of the Human Clone

We all have a moral responsibility to recognize the clone for what she is—a unique human person, with just as much human dignity as those of us who were conceived in more traditional ways.

*Nick Bostrom, "Human Reproductive Cloning
from the Perspective of the Future,"
December 27, 2002. www.nickbostrom.*

Is Cloning a Slippery Slope?

But perhaps clones are only the beginning. Might we not slide down a slippery slope into a dehumanized nightmare? Not as long as we remain capable of making nuanced moral judgments. And anyway, if this is a slippery slope, we are probably already on it. I suspect our path is more a slippery sidewalk. We may take a spill or two, but we'll get up, brush ourselves off, and continue on our way.

If human cloning is enough to bring down civilization, heaven help us, because throwing up obstacles to regenerative medicine is not going to save us. We are unraveling human biology, and many coming developments will be discomforting. But vaccines, antibiotics, organ transplants, and test-tube babies were each initially viewed as unnatural.

We can't avoid the coming advances and wouldn't want to if we could. They offer too many potential benefits. The real question is not how we handle embryonic stem cells or genetically altered foods or any other specific technology, but whether we will continue to embrace the possibilities of the future or will pull back and relinquish these explorations to other braver souls in other regions of the world.

We can choose to give up our leadership in medical research and watch the British or the Chinese set the course, but that will signal our decline. Our fall may take a while, but it will come.

In the aftermath of the World Trade Center attack and the anthrax mailings [in the fall of 2001], it is obvious that we face real enemies and dangers. Cloning and other advanced medical technologies, no matter how much they shake up our worldviews, are essentially on the side of life. They are intended to enhance our well being, not hurt us. The real dangers from biotech come not from this quarter, but from groups who have gone over to the dark side to weaponize ancient human enemies like plague and smallpox. We should not be so cavalier about stifling basic biomedical research, because ultimately, it may be what saves us.

Periodical Bibliography

The following articles have been selected to supplement the diverse views presented in this chapter.

Arthur L. Caplan "Politicians, Courts Must Allow Husband to Make Final Decision: The Time Has Come to Let Terri Schiavo Die," *Bioethics on MSNBC*, March 18, 2005. www.bioethics.net.

Kelly Eileen Dahlgren Childress "Genetics, Disability, and Ethics: Could Applied Technologies Lead to a New Eugenics?" *Journal of Women and Religion*, January 1, 2002.

Cynthia B. Cohen "Protestant Perspectives on the Uses of the New Reproductive Technologies," *Fordham Urban Law Journal*, November 1, 2002.

Michael Ennis "Culture of Strife: Both Stem Cell Research and Embryo Adoption Destroy the Building Blocks of Life. So Why Do Many Religious Conservatives Criticize One and Champion the Other?" *Texas Monthly*, October 2005.

Mary Johnson "No, It's Not About Terri Schiavo Anymore," *CommonDreams.org*, March 22, 2005. www-.commondreams.org.

Larry King, with Michael Schiavo and George Felos "Larry King Live: Interview," CNN, March 21, 2005. http://transcripts.cnn.com.

Daniel E. Lee "Physician-Assisted Suicide: A Conservative Critique of Intervention," *Hastings Center Report*, January/February 2003.

Joan Ryan "Choice in Life, Choice in Death," *San Francisco Chronicle*, February 9, 2003.

Christine A. Scheller "Ethics Interrupted: What Does It Mean When Even Embryonic Stem-Cell Researchers Have Some Qualms About Their Work?" *Christianity Today*, October 2005.

CHAPTER 4

Are American Corporations Ethical?

Chapter Preface

Profit certainly motivates action, but does it motivate moral action? For advocates of corporate social responsibility, corporate ethics is the foundation of a successful business. According to this view, companies that put ethics before profits succeed at every level: They generate goodwill among customers, improve morale among their workforce, benefit society overall, and realize increased profitability. However, not all economists and management theorists share this assessment. Recognizing that consumers purchase products and services because they need or want them, not because such purchases are good for society, some economists disagree with the notion that corporations should put ethics before profits. These critics assert that the pursuit of profits in itself is not unethical; indeed, they point out, the pursuit of profits indirectly advances the public good. Motivated by profits, companies develop needed products, satisfy consumers, and produce wealth for investors. The profits generated through commercial activity can then be used for social benefits such as helping the poor and protecting the environment.

At the center of many discussions about business ethics these days is Wal-Mart. As the largest company in the world and the leading employer in thirty-seven of the fifty states, Wal-Mart has increasingly come under scrutiny. By one estimate, Americans spend $26 million each hour at Wal-Mart, twenty-four hours a day, seven days a week. Detractors of Wal-Mart criticize the company for preventing workers from organizing unions, for violating workers' rights, for paying low wages, and for driving small businesses away with reduced pricing. In sum, critics say that the chain puts profits ahead of ethics to the detriment of society. Wal-Mart supporters, meanwhile, argue that the retailer provides exactly what American consumers want: convenience, variety, good quality merchandise, and low prices. These proponents assert that Wal-Mart provides jobs and investment within a community, which raises the overall standard of living, and often participates in charitable endeavors in the communities in which their stores are located. In sum, these commentators see Wal-Mart's dedication to profits as beneficial.

Vilified and praised, Wal-Mart epitomizes recent debates over corporate ethics. In the following chapter authors discuss a range of topics concerning the ethics of business in America. Whether emphasizing profits or ethics, American corporations have an increasing responsibility to be seen as good citizens.

> *"Ethics ... is no longer a luxury to be enjoyed by those companies blessed with strong, principled leadership. Today, ethics is a basic necessity."*

Corporations Must Focus on Improving Business Ethics

Andrew E. Reisman

Andrew E. Reisman is a consultant to leading companies worldwide on issues of ethics, compliance, and corporate governance. In the following viewpoint Reisman advocates corporate ethics as the foundation of a successful business. Reisman defines a new era in American business in which a strong code of ethical behavior is not a luxury but a basic necessity. He claims that ethical leadership sets the standard of behavior in a corporate culture.

As you read, consider the following questions:

1. Why does Reisman claim that a culture of ethics is a basic necessity for corporations?
2. What catchphrase from baseball does the author apply to business ethics?

3. What does Reisman believe is the factor most necessary to the development of an ethical corporate culture?

I t is easy to believe in the wake of seemingly incessant corporate scandals that business and ethics go together like instant and classic or like jumbo and shrimp. Yet, they must go together for ethical, business, and legal reasons.

The Sarbanes-Oxley Act [passed in 2002] tightened stock exchange listing requirements and increased enforcement activity by regulators. Results from these latest corporate scandals have solidified the need for strict compliance with both the letter and spirit of the law. Those listing requirements also require Codes of Ethics for public companies. Indeed, in April, the U.S. Sentencing Commission, an independent agency in the judicial branch that develops sentencing guidelines for U.S. judges, shifted its emphasis away from simple compliance to a more comprehensive culture of ethics and values alongside compliance. All of which makes one thing abundantly clear—no company can afford to be without a sense of "business ethics."

Ethics Is a Business Necessity

Ethics—and a corporate culture that stresses ethical behavior from the top down—is no longer a luxury to be enjoyed by those companies blessed with strong, principled leadership. Today, ethics is a basic necessity. A corporate culture without ethics is only a rogue employee away from potential catastrophe. Just ask anyone who worked at Enron.[1]

Or, better yet, ask Marjorie Doyle. As chief compliance officer for The DuPont Company, Doyle's job is to nurture and continually refresh an ethical culture—a challenge that's actually eased somewhat in recent years by the rash of misconduct and ensuing calamitous headlines.

1. At Enron shareholders and employees lost millions of dollars in investments and pensions after it became known in late 2001 that company executives had used fraudulent accounting, trading, and reporting practices to hide financial losses and falsely inflate the company's earnings.

"One thing I've been saying to our people," Doyle says, "is that we should be concerned about ethics and compliance just because it's the right thing to do—but oh, by the way, this does affect your bottom line. And, depending on where your culture is, it can be a real competitive advantage."

Doyle continues, "Your vendors, customers, and employees—all the people that keep you going—want to be associated with a company that's going to be around. They don't want to be putting all their eggs in a basket—whether they're a vendor or a customer or whatever—with an Enron, and then [they are] gone. Or, if you're an employee, and then your pension is gone."

Developing an Ethical Corporate Culture

Of course, this is easier said than done. Although the need for an ethical corporate culture is obvious, how you develop that culture is less so. Businesses are complex, with myriad competing influences originating from within the company and from outside sources.

It is one thing for an individual or a company to lean against a tide of unethical behavior, but how do you change the tide altogether? How do you get everyone in the company on board, and once they are on board, how do you keep them there in the face of outside influences—vendors, partners, customers, and competitors—who may not share your zeal for the company's ethical welfare?

Certainly, what once may have seemed adequate will no longer suffice. It is not enough to write a lofty mission statement and hang it behind glass on the CEO's wall. Today, a company's mission statement has to actually guide the mission, influencing company policy both large and small. Likewise, leadership cannot simply pay lip service to a code of conduct that stays hidden away in the employee handbook. Regulators are justifiably skeptical of "paper programs." After all, Enron itself had 60-plus-pages for their code of conduct

THE WALL STREET JOURNAL

"We make money the old-fashioned way... first we undercut the competition into bankruptcy, and then we jack up the prices!"

that was beautifully written and completely ineffectual. Everyone in a company, from the boardroom to the break room, must know that code and live by its principles. . . .

An Ethical Ecosystem

Business ethics can no longer be seen as an individual pursuit, either for the people who make up a company or for the company as a whole. "Everything affects everything," in the words of former Baltimore Orioles manager Earl Weaver.

Think of a rainforest. The tallest trees spread out to form a canopy, providing shade and shelter and dictating the behavior of all the animal and plant life below. Meanwhile, smaller plants thrive in the interior, relying on the taller trees for support and sustenance by providing food for the animals and insects. Those insects distribute seeds to keep the forest growing and diverse. And on the jungle floor, bacteria turn fallen leaves and branches into nutrients that help keep the tallest trees alive. It is a delicate balance, and if you take away any part of it—even the tiniest bacteria—there are profound ramifications to all of the other interdependent forms of life.

The same principle applies to an ethical ecosystem. Just as one rogue element can damage a company, so can one rogue company damage an entire industry. However, at the same time, the largest companies form a canopy above an industry, dictating the way all business is conducted. If those tall trees establish a strong ethical paradigm, then the ethical elements below can survive and thrive, squeezing out the rogues in the process and keeping the industry leaders—and the industry as a whole—healthy.

Charlie Chadwick, vice president of contracts for BAE Systems North America, says it is like tossing a pebble into a pond. The ripples, he points out, expand well beyond the immediate point of impact.

"The actions of individual employees who are held accountable and responsible for their conduct have ripple effects," Chadwick says. He continues:

They affect those with whom the employees most immediately interface. It is absolutely true that peer pressure is a wonderful device, both for good and for ill. If the employees individually take responsibility—if they believe they are accountable and they are actually held accountable for their actions being ethical—that influence goes around them and those concentric rings come into play. It keeps expanding out beyond their immediate peer group to the company as a whole.

"It's probably not too exaggerated," Chadwick says, "to say that it expands out potentially to the community, to the culture as a whole, and to the industry." . . .

Nurturing Nature

[There is] only one place to start the process of nurturing a robust ethical ecosystem, and that's with a robust ethical corporate culture.

The process is by now familiar to most in the corporate world. Companies have to make a concerted effort to hire the best people, and to foster a more satisfying and productive work environment. Open dialogue must be legitimized and encouraged, and the trust of employees must be maintained.

Corporations are really cultures—groups of people who either work together or work apart. A company's values must permeate the entire operation, and ethical behavior and responsible conduct must be both encouraged and rewarded. Once all this is in place, the ethical ecosystem can begin to function.

But of course, it can't end there. Those values must constantly be reinforced, and the tone has to be set at the top through both word and conduct. According to a 2003 business ethics survey conducted by the Society for Human Resources Management and the Ethics Resource Center, the number-one source of pressure on corporate employees to compromise the company's standards isn't naked self-interest, or even schedule pressures—it's the boss himself. Leadership counts. . . .

Ethics and Good Economics

Although creating and sustaining an ethical ecosystem requires considerable, ongoing investment and nurturing, it also provides a prodigious return as well. With so many outside factors at play, it is impossible for a company to maintain a healthy ethical culture without stretching that culture out past the corporate walls. But the ecosystem model is important for an even more basic reason, says Chadwick—it's necessary for industry to function at all.

"I'm a contracts guy," he says, "and every contract carries an implied covenant of good faith and fair dealing. The presumption is that you act in good faith. And eventually, if no one can assume that, commerce is crippled."

Doyle points out that, in an ethical ecosystem, principles do not merely coexist with profits, they in fact enable them. There are, she says, always going to be competitors who will mimic your best products and processes. But one thing that cannot be copied is a strong reputation. And that reputation can be a distinct edge in a competitive marketplace.

"It is very important to let your customers know that you are in fact an ethical company," Doyle says. "Let your vendors know because this gives you an advantage. They may take less money to work with you rather than with some other company because there's more security there."

"More and more," she says, "folks in the ecosystem, whether it's customers or your suppliers, are looking for someone who's going to be ethical—and therefore be around."

An enduring corporate reputation has become increasingly valuable and more central in the eyes of employees, the markets, and other constituencies.

Instead of the Enrons of the world grabbing headlines, we are finally beginning to see the good news of companies such as DuPont, BAE Systems, and Kennecott—companies that have long been admired for doing what's right—as they receive credit for their place at the heart of an ethical business ecosystem.

> *"If self-interest ... inadvertently serves the public good, then it is easy to see why society can prosper even if people are not always driven by benevolence."*

Corporations Must Focus on Profits

Economist

The Economist *is a British weekly publication that espouses free trade and free markets but often supports liberal social views. In the following viewpoint the* Economist *asserts that self-interest drives commerce and that the pursuit of profits advances the public good. When companies pursue profits, the magazine maintains, they create needed goods, spurn innovation, and produce wealth, which can then be used for social benefits such as protecting the environment. The* Economist *argues against corporate social responsibility (CSR) models that emphasize corporate citizenship over profits, noting that CSR proponents often seek increased regulation of industry, which the magazine claims harms the public by restricting industry's ability to turn a profit.*

As you read, consider the following questions:

1. How does the *Economist* distinguish greed from self-interest?

2. In the *Economist*'s analysis, how is the public good reflected in the prices of products and services?

3. Why does the author maintain that economic development is not necessarily bad for the environment?

A dam Smith, you might say, wrote the book on corporate social responsibility [CSR]. It is entitled, *Wealth of Nations*.

> Every individual necessarily labours to render the annual revenue of the society as great as he can. He generally, indeed, neither intends to promote the public interest, nor knows how much he is promoting it . . . he intends only his own gain, and he is in this, as in many other cases, led by an invisible hand to promote an end which was no part of his intention. Nor is it always the worse for the society that it was no part of it. By pursuing his own interest he frequently promotes that of the society more effectually than when he really intends to promote it. I have never known much good done by those who affected to trade for the public good.

> It is not from the benevolence of the butcher, the brewer, or the baker, that we expect our dinner, but from their regard to their own interest. We address ourselves, not to their humanity but to their self-love, and never talk to them of our own necessities but of their advantages.

Smith did not worship selfishness. He regarded benevolence as admirable, as a great virtue, and he saw the instinct for sympathy towards one's fellow man as the foundation on which civilised conduct is built (he wrote another book about this: *The Theory of Moral Sentiments*). But his greatest economic insight—and indeed the greatest single insight yielded by the discipline of economics—was that benevolence was not in fact necessary to advance the public interest, so long as people were free to engage with each other in voluntary economic interaction. That is fortunate, he pointed out, since benevolence is often in short supply. Self-interest, on the other hand, is not.

If self-interest, guided as though by an invisible hand, inadvertently serves the public good, then it is easy to see why society can prosper even if people are not always driven by benevolence. It is because Smith was right about self-interest and the public interest that communism failed and capitalism worked.

The Harmony of Private Interest and Public Interest

Most advocates of CSR, especially those who run giant international corporations, have probably read some economics in their time. Many of the officials at the United Nations, World Bank and OECD [Organisation for Economic Cooperation and Development] who argue in favour of CSR have advanced degrees in the subject from the best universities. Yet they have apparently failed to grasp this most basic and necessary insight of the entire discipline. Through the action of Smith's invisible hand, the private search for *profit* does advance the public interest. There is no need for thought-leaders in CSR armed with initiatives and compacts to bring this about.

Smith was a genius because this harmony of private interest and public interest is not at all obvious—and yet, at the same time, once it is pointed out, the idea is instantly simple and plausible. This is especially so if you think not about self-interested individuals but about *profit*-seeking companies. The value that people attach to the goods and services they buy from companies is shown by what they are willing to pay for them. The costs of producing those goods and services are a measure of what society has to surrender to consume those things. If what people pay exceeds the cost, society has gained—and the company has turned a *profit*. The bigger the gain for society, the bigger the *profit*. So *profits* are a guide (by no means a perfect one, but a guide nonetheless) to the value that companies create for society.

Does this mean that Gordon Gekko, the odious protagonist of the movie, *Wall Street*, was right to say that "greed is good"? No: greed and self-interest are not the same thing, as Mr. Gekko discovered in that movie. Greed, in the ordinary meaning of the word, is not rational or calculating. Freely indulged, it makes you fat and drives you into bankruptcy. The kind of self-interest that advances the public good is rational and enlightened. Rational, calculating self-interest makes a person, or a firm, worry about its reputation for honesty and fair dealing, for paying debts and honouring agreements. It looks beyond the short term and plans ahead. It considers sacrifices today for the sake of gains tomorrow, or five years from now. It makes good neighbours.

Morally, also, there is a world of difference between greed and self-interest. The first, even if it were not self-defeating, would still be a gross perversion of the second. Failing to see this distinction, and thus concluding without further thought that private enterprise is tainted, is a kind of ethical stupidity. Greed is ugly. There is nothing ignoble, in contrast, about a calm and moderate desire to advance one's own welfare, married (as it is in most people) to a sympathetic regard for the well-being of others. And, as Smith pointed out, rational self-interest also happens to make the world go round.

A Faulty Premise

The premise that CSR advocates never question is in fact wrong. It is an error to suppose that *profit*-seeking, as such, fails to advance the public good, and that special efforts to give something back to society are needed to redeem it.

However, as already noted, *profit* succeeds as an indicator of value creation, and as a signal that draws new investment to socially useful purposes, only under certain circumstances. It cannot be taken for granted that these conditions will always be satisfied.

One main requirement is that firms are in competition with each other. The *profits* that a monopoly can extract from the economy are a measure of market power, not social gain. And monopoly *profits* may not serve as an effective signal for new investment if economic barriers of one kind or another hamper competition by keeping new entrants off the monopolist's turf.

Oddly enough, business leaders who voice their commitment to good corporate citizenship rarely demand the removal of barriers to competition in their industries—a measure that would almost invariably serve the public interest. Manufacturers are far more likely to call for import barriers to be raised against their foreign competitors than they are to call for existing tariffs or other barriers to come down. Producers of all manner of goods and services are more likely to call for the introduction of licences and controls to protect their existing positions in their markets than to demand that newcomers should be permitted and even encouraged to contest those markets.

And CSR often helps them in this. Although it is true that many business leaders mean what they say about good corporate citizenship, and speak up for CSR in good faith, CSR is nonetheless far more often invoked as a rationale for anticompetitive practices than as a reason to bolster competition. Incumbent firms or professions seem to find it easier to comply with burdensome regulations if they know that those rules are deterring new entrants. That is why, often in the name of CSR, incumbent businesses are so given to calling for rules and standards to be harmonised and extended, both at home and abroad.

For the good of the public, you understand, barristers are opposed to reforms that would allow solicitors to appear more often as advocates in English courts (their training just isn't up to it). For the safety of the consumer, American pharmaceutical companies insist, extraordinary precautions must be taken before drugs can be imported from Canada (heaven knows what the Canadians, a devil-may-care sort of people, put into those pills). For the good of the world's poor, industrial-country manufacturers believe, goods should not be imported from countries where employees have to work long hours for low pay and without statutory vacations (that is unfair trade).

A great deal of economic regulation makes sense for one reason or another. But it is striking that business leaders—especially, it seems, those who speak up most enthusiastically for CSR—call for regulation that restricts competition far more often than they call for regulation that strengthens it. This prompts the thought that the design of economic regulation is best left to governments, rather than to corporate citizens, however enlightened.

Social Prices

A second condition must be met before one can be sure that private enterprise in competitive markets is advancing the public good. Prices need to reflect true social costs and benefits. Many transactions, however, have side-effects—externalities, as they are called. Where they do, private costs and benefits diverge from public costs and benefits. Sometimes externalities are positive. If your neighbour repaints his house, that may increase the value of yours; since he fails to capture all the gains created by his spending, he may repaint his house less frequently than would be best for society at large—or, in this case, for your end of the street. Markets tend to undersupply goods that involve positive externalities.

Externalities can also be negative. The classic instance is a polluting factory. The owners of the factory and the customers for its goods do not have to bear the full costs of the pollution that comes out of its smokestacks. Failing to take that into account, the market sets the price of the factory's goods too low.

Who Gave Us More?

Who did more for the world, Michael Milken or Mother Teresa?

This seems like a no-brainer. Milken is the greedy junk-bond king. One year, his firm paid him $550 million. Then he went to jail for breaking securities laws. Mother Teresa is the nun who spent her lifetime helping the poor and died without a penny. Her good deeds live on even after her death; several thousand sisters now continue the charities she began. At first glance, of course Mother Teresa did more for the world.

But it's not so simple. Milken's selfish pursuit of profit helped a lot of people, too. Think about it: By pioneering a new way for companies to raise money, Milken created millions of jobs. The ignorant media sneered at "junk bonds," but Milken's innovative use of them meant exciting new ideas flourished. . . .

It was [David] Kelley who came up with the idea of comparing Milken and Mother Teresa. "People look at the two, and they say, 'That's absurd. Mother Teresa was a moral hero, and he was a criminal. Michael Milken didn't suffer. He didn't go into the slums.' . . . But I say, what's so good about suffering? Look at the value [these two] people created. And on that scale, I have no trouble—Michael Milken [did more for the world]." Kelley wasn't even counting the hundreds of millions Milken donated to education and medical research. He considered only what Milken created by pursuing profit.

John Stossel, Give Me a Break, *2004.*

Demand for the product is stronger than it should be. Goods that involve negative externalities tend to be over-supplied.

This kind of argument is invoked to make sense of "sustainable development" and the claims pressed on business by that idea. Prices are wrong, the argument goes, so markets are failing. Pollution, including the accumulation of greenhouse gases, is not priced into the market, so there is too much of it. Impending shortages of natural resources are not priced into the market, so those resources are consumed too rapidly. The value of wilderness, either for its beauty or for its stocks of endangered species, is not priced into the market, so too much of it gets cemented over.

Whether the pattern of consumption based on these false prices is sustainable is really beside the point. Some patterns of consumption could be indefinitely sustained but still be wrong, causing mounting damage as far ahead as one can see. Others might indeed be unsustainable, meaning bound to be halted at some point, yet not be wrong, as when the approaching exhaustion of a raw material leads to the invention of a substitute. "Sustainability" has a nice ring to it, but it is not the issue. The question is whether false prices are causing big economic mistakes—and, if so, what might be done about that.

Many market prices do diverge from the corresponding "shadow prices" that would direct resources to their socially best uses. In many cases, the divergence is big enough to warrant government action—a point which all governments have taken on board, sometimes to a fault. All industrial-country governments intervene in their economies. In principle, much of this intervention aims to mitigate the misallocation of resources caused by externalities and other kinds of market failure. But it is important to keep a sense of proportion about the supposed unreliability of market signals.

So far as environmental externalities are concerned, most leading advocates of CSR seem to be in the grip of a grossly exaggerated environmental pessimism. The claim that economic growth is necessarily bad for the environment is an article of faith in the CSR movement. But this idea is simply wrong.

Natural resources are not running out, if you measure effective supply in relation to demand. The reason is that scarcity raises prices, which spurs innovation: new sources are found, the efficiency of extraction goes up, existing supplies are used more economically, and substitutes are invented. In 1970, global reserves of copper were estimated at 280m tonnes; during the next 30 years about 270m tonnes were consumed. Where did estimated reserves of copper stand at the turn of the century? Not at 10m tonnes, but at 340m. Available supplies have surged, and, it so happens, demand per unit of economic activity has been falling: copper is being replaced in many of its main industrial applications by other materials (notably, fibre-optic cable instead of copper wire for telecommunications).

Copper, therefore, is unlikely ever to run out—and if it did, in some very distant future, it would be unlikely by then to matter. The same is true for other key minerals. Reserves of bauxite in 1970 were 5.3 billion tonnes; the amount consumed between 1970 and 2000 was around 3 billion tonnes; reserves by the end of the century stood at 25 billion tonnes. Or take energy. Oil reserves in 1970: 580 billion barrels. Oil consumed between 1970 and the turn of the century: 690 billion barrels. Oil reserves in 2000: 1,050 billion barrels. And so on.

The Colour of Gloom

What about pollution? On the whole, rich countries are less polluted than poor countries, not more. The reason is that wealth increases both the demand for a healthier environment and the means to bring it about. Environmental regulation has been necessary to achieve this, to be sure, because pollution is indeed an externality. But it is not true that the problem has been left unattended in the rich world, that things are therefore getting worse, and that CSR initiatives have to rise to the challenge of dealing with this neglect.

Strong environmental protection is already in place in Europe and the United States. In some cases, no doubt, it needs to be strengthened further. In some other cases, most likely, it is already too strong. Overall, the evidence fails to show systematic neglect, or any tendency, once government regulation is taken into account, for economic growth to make things worse.

How much of an exception to this is global warming? Potentially, as many CSR advocates say, a very important one. Emissions of greenhouse gases are causing stocks of carbon in the atmosphere to grow rapidly. Almost all climate scientists expect this to raise temperatures to some unknown extent during the coming decades. If temperatures rise towards the upper end of current projections, the environmental damage will be great.

Yet the world still lacks an effective regime for global carbon abatement. This is not so much because the United States has refused to support the Kyoto agreement [to reduce greenhouse gas emissions] as because that agreement is deeply flawed in any case—but this is beside the point. Global warming is a potentially very significant externality that governments up to now have failed to address properly.

Another such case is excessive encroachment on wilderness areas. Once a wilderness has been lost, it cannot be replaced—and, unlike for copper or oil, there will never be a substitute. Governments in many rich and poor countries are neglecting this issue.

But on questions such as these, where governments are, it seems, leaving significant market failures unaddressed, the question for businesses is whether CSR can do anything useful to bridge the gap. Many companies at the forefront of the

CSR movement have embarked on initiatives of their own, aimed, for example, at reducing greenhouse-gas emissions or at protecting wilderness areas.

These would need to be judged case by case, to see whether particular policies were instances of "good management" (as when an oil company invests profitably in alternative fuels, anticipating both shifts in consumer demand and forthcoming taxes on carbon), "borrowed virtue" (for example, creating private wilderness reserves at shareholders' expense), "pernicious CSR" (blocking competition in the name of specious environmental goals) or "delusional CSR" (increasing emissions of greenhouse gases in order to conserve raw materials that are not in diminishing supply).

There will be good and bad. As a general rule, however, correcting market failures is best left to government. Businesses cannot be trusted to get it right, partly because they lack the wherewithal to frame intelligent policy in these areas. Aside from the implausibility of expecting the unco-ordinated actions of thousands of private firms to yield a coherent optimising policy on global warming, say, there is also what you might call the constitutional issue. The right policy on global warming is not clear-cut even at the global level, to say nothing of the national level or the level of the individual firm or consumer. Devising such a policy, and sharing the costs equitably, is a political challenge of the first order. Settling such questions exceeds both the competence and the proper remit of private enterprise.

> "When all's said and done, Wal-Mart
> employs lots of people; provides heaps
> of things you need in one place at the
> lowest prices you'll find; and gives mil-
> lions to charities every year."

Wal-Mart Benefits Americans

Karen De Coster

*In the following viewpoint Karen De Coster defends Wal-Mart
against some common accusations. Despite claims that the chain
store drives down wages, according to De Coster, Wal-Mart's
wages are not out of line with other retail stores. Critics also say
that Wal-Mart drives out smaller competitors by keeping prices
low, but De Coster contends that low prices are exactly what
consumers want. In addition, according to De Coster, Wal-Mart
retail centers offer consumers convenience, value, and an array of
quality merchandise. De Coster is an economist, accountant, and
freelance writer.*

As you read, consider the following questions:

1. What factors does De Coster say contribute to Wal-
   Mart's reputation for paying low wages?
2. What does the author find implausible about the theory
   that Wal-Mart sets artificially low prices to drive out
   competition in small towns?

3. According to De Coster, what evidence indicates that Americans love Wal-Mart?

T he accusations against Wal-Mart are numerous, and they include: paying overseas workers too little; not paying benefits to part-time workers; refusing to sell items that don't fall within its criteria for being "family-oriented"; not giving enough back to the community; and discriminating against women. All the accusations leveled against Wal-Mart can be applied to just about any large corporation in America, as frequently is the case. For example, Kathie Lee Gifford was almost run out of the country for indirectly giving jobs to otherwise unemployable, Third World workers.

In addition, most retail and service sector employees still do not get paid full job benefits, so what makes Wal-Mart so distinctive in that case? What's more, Wal-Mart management has indeed made decisions to refrain from selling certain items that did not live up to its moral standards—including certain music CDs and a brand of barbecue sauce sold by a man who promoted his Confederate heritage—but what's wrong with a private company exercising its own moral discretion according to its stated values? Accordingly, the marvelous ways of the free market allow us to move on elsewhere for our purchases when we are dissatisfied with what we perceive as corporate nonsense.

Wal-Mart is an employer that pays relatively low wages compared to most jobs or careers, and that engenders a sense of loathing from people getting paid those wages. But Wal-Mart is not unlike any other retailer in the respect that it, for the most part, provides jobs and not careers. Other gigantic corporations such as General Electric or General Motors, on the other hand, employ executives, college graduates, and skilled laborers, so they avoid much of the wage-related scrutiny given to retail employers. Add to that the labor union organizers' inability to unionize Wal-Mart and you have the perfect recipe for resentment and scorn.

The Impact of Wal-Mart on the Marketplace

The overriding charges one comes across amid the many Wal-Mart rants are "too large" and "too powerful." Thus it's just more anti-industry, anti-free market claptrap. Along with that are the hoots and hollers about this great chain "destroying small towns" by way of buying property in rural areas and opening its doors to townsfolk so they have access to convenient, one-stop shopping, an ample supply of products, and unbeatable prices.

However, there is one prevailing phenomenon that makes Wal-Mart a unique target for contempt and that is its "bigness." Americans, generally speaking, like to attack bigness. There are things associated with bigness that Americans aren't keen on, like clout and domination.

In fact, the favorite indictment of Wal-Mart is that they dominate the market wherever they go and sell goods at prices that are too low (gasp!). This in turn—say the naysayers—drives small, local competitors out of business because they can't compete with Wal-Mart's pricing or product selection.

Suppose it's true that Wal-Mart went around opening giant stores in small towns, pricing goods below their own cost long enough to drive local stores out of business. Even if this were correct, Wal-Mart would only be selling its own property. Suppose you want to sell a house you inherited, and quickly. Should you not be allowed to set the price as low as you want?

The theory goes that Wal-Mart could then set prices high, and make monopoly profits. How plausible is this, really? First, Wal-Mart executives would have to be able to see the future—they'd have to know about how long it would take to drive everyone out of business in advance, and know whether they could afford to price goods below cost for long enough to corner the market. Then, through trial and error, they'd have to find the point at which they could set prices low

The Legacy of Wal-Mart

[Now] it's time for me to forget about all that's past and think about what I really want the legacy of Wal-Mart to be in the future. I'd like to believe that as Wal-Mart continues to thrive and grow, it can come to live up to what someone once called us: the Lighthouse of the Ozarks. Only I hope we can spread the concept further than our home region here in the foothills because we're really a national company now. For Wal-Mart to maintain its position in the hearts of our customers, we have to study more ways we can give something back to our communities. I'm tremendously proud of the things we've done. . . . And we're already studying ways we can go further to stay involved, to be more socially conscious all around. . . . Our country desperately needs a revolution in education, and I hope Wal-Mart can contribute at some level, if for no other reason than selfish ones. Without a strong educational system, the very free enterprise system that allows a Wal-Mart or an IBM or a Procter & Gamble to appear on the scene and strengthen our nation's economy simply won't work. You may have trouble believing it, but every time we've tested the old saying, it has paid off for us in spades: the more you give, the more you get.

Sam Walton, Made in America: My Story, *1992.*

enough to keep customers from driving to another town, but high enough to recoup the losses from the earlier below-cost pricing.

It gets less plausible the more you think about it: The smaller the town, the easier it would be to drive competitors out of business. Then again, a town small enough for this would be small enough to have bitter memories of the pricing strategy and small enough to boycott Wal-Mart before the strategy succeeded. And a very small town would not support a giant Wal-Mart anyway. The larger the town, the less feasible it would be to drive others out of business in that town— Wal-Mart would have to drive their prices far below those of large grocery and department stores, which would be much more difficult.

Further, where is there evidence of Wal-Mart ever driving up prices after becoming established in a market? Wal-Mart has indeed set prices low enough to drive mom & pop stores out of business all over the country and kept the prices that low forever. Yet a journalist for the *Cleveland Scene* said about Wal-Mart's pricing policy: "That's 100 million shoppers a week lured by 'Always Low Prices.'" Lured—as if consumers really don't want low prices; they are just tricked into thinking they do!

Pricing in a Free Market Economy

In a free market, large suppliers of nearly everything will drive most small suppliers out of business. The only people who can afford to do business on a small scale are people at the top of their fields or in a niche: McDonald's has to keep prices low, and economies of scale do this, while Brennan's restaurant in New Orleans can keep prices high. People who produce house paint and wallpaper must compete on price with other suppliers, while famous artists can keep their prices high. General Motors must keep prices low, while Rolls-Royce doesn't have to.

Nobody complains that there aren't family auto manufacturers, but the powerful farmers' political lobby makes sure we pay inflated prices to keep inefficient farmers in business. Of course, giant agribusinesses don't complain that their weaker competition is kept in the market, because the giant agribusinesses enjoy the inflated prices just as do the family farmers, some of whom are paid to leave their fields fallow.

Nobody complains that there aren't family pharmaceutical manufacturers, but people complain when Wal-Mart drives a corner drug store out of business. Yet if the corner drug store owners had the same political lobbying power farmers have, you can bet we'd be paying $20 for Q-tips.

Wal-Mart Improves Rural Life

If the truth be told, Wal-Mart improves the lives of people in rural areas because it gives them access to a lifestyle that they otherwise would not have—a gigantic store showcasing the world's greatest choice of products from groceries to music to automotive products. When it comes to prices and service, try finding 70% off clearances at your local mom-and-pop store or try going to that same store and returning shoes you've worn for three months for a full-price refund with no questions asked.

On the whole, if one doesn't like Wal-Mart and finds it to be of greater utility to support their local mom-and-pop stores for an assortment of cultural and non-economic reasons, then they may do so. If consumers wish to obstruct the development of a Wal-Mart store in their small town, they have scores of non-bullying options to pick from in order to try and persuade their fellow townsfolk that a new Wal-Mart is not the best option.

Still, it is not always easy to convince folks to eschew ultra-convenience for the sake of undefined, moral purposes. Consumers most often shop with their wallet, not with political precepts. For that reason, the anti-Wal-Mart crowd uses political coercion and an assortment of anti-private property decrees—such as zoning manipulation—in order to stave off the construction of a new Wal-Mart store in their town.

Hating Wal-Mart is the equivalent of hating Bill Gates. Sam Walton had a grandiose vision for himself, and sought to realize that vision by providing something people want—low prices. He has done every bit as much for your lifestyle as Bill Gates.

Benefits of Wal-Mart Shopping

Families who shop carefully at Wal-Mart can actually budget more for investing, children's college funds, or entertainment. And unlike other giant corporations, Wal-Mart stores around the country make an attempt to provide a friendly atmosphere by spending money to hire greeters, who are often people who would have difficulty finding any other job. This is a friendly, partial solution to shoplifting problems; the solution K-mart applied ("Hey, what's in that bag?") didn't work as well.

It's interesting to observe that the consumers who denounce Wal-Mart are often the same folks who take great joy in reaping the rewards of corporate bigness, such as saving money with sales, clearances, and coupons, being able to engage in comparative shopping, and taking advantage of generous return policies. When all's said and done, Wal-Mart employs lots of people; provides heaps of things you need in one place at the lowest prices you'll find; and gives millions to charities every year. Add up the charitable giving of all the mom & pop stores in the country and it probably won't equal that of one giant corporation.

To be sure, if Americans didn't love Wal-Mart so much it wouldn't be sitting at the top of the 2002 Fortune 500 with $219 billion in revenues. And we do love Wal-Mart. We love it because it gives us variety and abundance. We love it because it saves us time and wrangling. And we love it because no matter where we are, it's always there when we need it.

> *"Wal-Mart's success has meant downward pressures on wages and benefits, rampant violations of basic workers' rights, and threats to the standard of living in communities across the country."*

Wal-Mart Harms Americans

George Miller

George Miller is a Democratic congressman from California. He is on the House Education and the Workforce Committee and also serves on the House Resources Committee. In the following viewpoint Miller criticizes Wal-Mart for preventing workers from organizing unions, violating workers' rights, paying low wages, and making health care unavailable to or unaffordable for its workers. Miller charges that U.S. taxpayers subsidize wages at Wal-Mart because its underpaid employees seek government assistance to help with their housing, food, and medical costs.

As you read, consider the following questions:

1. According to Miller, how do Wal-Mart's wages compare with wages paid to employees in the supermarket industry overall?

2. Who is eligible to enroll in Wal-Mart's health insurance plan, according to the author?

George Miller, "Everyday Low Wages: The Hidden Price We All Pay for Wal-Mart," http://edworkforce.house.gov, February 16, 2004.

3. What does Miller estimate is the cost to federal taxpayers of one Wal-Mart store?

The retail giant Wal-Mart has become the nation's largest created private sector employer with an estimated 1.2 million employees. The company's annual revenues now amount to 2 percent of the U.S. Gross Domestic Product. Wal-Mart's success is attributed to its ability to charge low prices in megastores offering everything from toys and furniture to groceries. While charging low prices obviously has some consumer benefits, mounting evidence from across the country indicates that these benefits come at a steep price for American workers, U.S. labor laws, and community living standards.

Wal-Mart is undercutting labor standards at home and abroad, while those federal officials charged with protecting labor standards have been largely indifferent. Public outcry against Wal-Mart's labor practices has been answered by the company with a cosmetic response. Wal-Mart has attempted to offset its labor record with advertising campaigns utilizing employees (who are euphemistically called "associates") to attest to Wal-Mart's employment benefits and support of local communities. Nevertheless—whether the issue is basic organizing rights of workers, or wages, or health benefits, or working conditions, or trade policy—Wal-Mart has come to represent the lowest common denominator in the treatment of working people. . . .

Workers' Organizing Rights

The United States recognizes workers' right to organize unions. Government employers generally may not interfere with public sector employees' freedom of association. In the private sector, workers' right to organize is protected by the National Labor Relations Act. Internationally, this right is recognized as a core labor standard and a basic human right.

Wal-Mart's record on the right to organize recently achieved international notoriety. On January 14, 2004, the International Confederation of Free Trade Unions (ICFTU), an organization representing 151 million workers in 233 affiliated unions around the world, issued a report on U.S. labor standards. Wal-Mart's rampant violations of workers' rights figured prominently. In the last few years, well over 100 unfair labor practice charges have been lodged against Wal-Mart throughout the country, with 43 charges filed in 2002 alone. Since 1995, the U.S. government has been forced to issue at least 60 complaints against Wal-Mart at the National Labor Relations Board. Wal-Mart's labor law violations range from illegally firing workers who attempt to organize a union to unlawful surveillance, threats, and intimidation of employees who dare to speak out. . . .

Wal-Mart's aggressive anti-union activity, along with the nation's weak labor laws, have kept the largest private sector employer in the U.S. union-free. . . .

Low Wages

By keeping unions at bay, Wal-Mart keeps its wages low—even by general industry standards. The average supermarket employee makes $10.35 per hour. Sales clerks at Wal-Mart, on the other hand, made only $8.23 per hour on average, or $13,861 per year, in 2001. Some estimate that average "associate" salaries range from $7.50 to $8.50 per hour. With an average on-the-clock workweek of 32 hours, many workers take home less than $1,000 per month. Even the higher estimate of a $13,861 annual salary fell below the 2001 federal poverty line of $14,630 for a family of three. About one-third of Wal-Mart's employees are part-time, restricting their access to benefits. These low wages, to say the least, complicate employees' ability to obtain essential benefits, such as health care coverage. . . .

Off-the-Clock Work

While wages are low at Wal-Mart, too often employees are not paid at all. The Fair Labor Standards Act (FLSA), along with state wage and hour laws, requires hourly employees to be paid for all time actually worked at no less than a minimum wage and at time-and-a-half for all hours worked over 40 in a week. These labor laws have posed a particular obstacle for Wal-Mart. As of December 2002, there were thirty-nine class-action lawsuits against the company in thirty states, claiming tens of millions of dollars in back pay for hundreds of thousands of Wal-Mart employees.

In 2001, Wal-Mart forked over $50 million in unpaid wages to 69,000 workers in Colorado. These wages were paid only after the workers filed a class action lawsuit. Wal-Mart had been working the employees off-the-clock. The company also paid $500,000 to 120 workers in Gallup, New Mexico, who filed a lawsuit over unpaid work. . . .

Many observers blame the wage-and-hour problems at Wal-Mart on pressure placed on managers to keep labor costs down. In 2002, operating costs for Wal-Mart were just 16.6 percent of total sales, compared to a 20.7 percent average for the retail industry as a whole. Wal-Mart reportedly awards bonuses to its employees based on earnings. With other operating and inventory costs set by higher level management, store managers must turn to wages to increase profits. While Wal-Mart expects those managers to increase sales each year, it expects the labor costs to be cut by two-tenths of a percentage point each year as well.

Reports from former Wal-Mart managers seem to corroborate this dynamic. Joyce Moody, a former manager in Alabama and Mississippi, told the *New York Times* that Wal-Mart "threatened to write up managers if they didn't bring the payroll in low enough." Depositions in wage and hour lawsuits reveal that company headquarters leaned on management to keep their labor costs at 8 percent of sales or less, and managers in turn leaned on assistant managers to work their employees off-the-clock or simply delete time from employee time sheets. . . .

Wal-Mart's Power Brings Responsibility

It is inconceivable that Wal-Mart, king of counting the financial cost, is unaware of the human cost of wage levels and working conditions in its suppliers' businesses. Wal-Mart's power comes with responsibility to pay just wages. With hundreds of thousands of Wal-Mart employees below poverty-level income, corporate contributions to community and charity are not enough.

Brian Bolton, Sojourners, *February 2004.*

Unaffordable or Unavailable Health Care

Fewer than half—between 41 and 46 percent—of Wal-Mart's employees are insured by the company's health care plan, compared nationally to 66 percent of employees at large firms like Wal-Mart who receive health benefits from their employer. In recent years, the company increased obstacles for its workers to access its health care plan.

In 2002, Wal-Mart increased the waiting period for enrollment eligibility from 90 days to 6 months for full-time employees. Part-time employees must wait 2 years before they may enroll in the plan, and they may not purchase coverage for their spouses or children. The definition of part-time was changed from 28 hours or less per week to less than 34 hours per week. At the time, approximately one-third of Wal-Mart's workforce was part-time. By comparison, nationally, the average waiting period for health coverage for employees at large firms like Wal-Mart was 1.3 months.

The Wal-Mart plan itself shifts much of the health care costs onto employees. In 1999, employees paid 36 percent of the costs. In 2001, the employee burden rose to 42 percent. Nationally, large-firm employees pay on average 16 percent of the premium for health insurance. Unionized grocery workers typically pay nothing. Studies show that much of the decline in employer-based health coverage is due to shifts of premium costs from employers to employees.

Moreover, Wal-Mart employees who utilize their health care confront high deductibles and co-payments. A single worker could end up spending around $6,400 out-of-pocket—about 45 percent of her annual full-time salary—before seeing a single benefit from the health plan.

According to an AFL-CIO report issued in October 2003, the employees' low wages and Wal-Mart's cost-shifting render health insurance unaffordable, particularly for those employees with families. Even under the Wal-Mart plan with the highest deductible ($1,000)—and therefore with the lowest employee premium contribution—it would take an $8 per hour employee, working 34 hours per week, almost one-and-a-half months of pre-tax earnings to pay for one year of family coverage. . . .

Low Wages Mean High Costs to Taxpayers

Because Wal-Mart wages are generally not living wages, the company uses taxpayers to subsidize its labor costs. While [a] California study showed how much taxpayers were subsidizing Wal-Mart on health care alone [$20.5 million in California], the total costs to taxpayers for Wal-Mart's labor policies are much greater.

The Democratic Staff of the Committee on Education and the Workforce estimates that one 200-person Wal-Mart store may result in a cost to federal taxpayers of $420,750 per year—

about $2,103 per employee. Specifically, the low wages result in the following additional public costs being passed along to taxpayers:

- $36,000 a year for free and reduced lunches for just 50 qualifying Wal-Mart families.

- $42,000 a year for Section 8 housing assistance, assuming 3 percent of the store employees qualify for such assistance, at $6,700 per family.

- $125,000 a year for federal tax credits and deductions for low-income families, assuming 50 employees are heads of household with a child and 50 are married with two children.

- $100,000 a year for the additional Title I expenses, assuming 50 Wal-Mart families qualify with an average of 2 children.

- $108,000 a year for the additional federal health care costs of moving into state children's health insurance programs (S-CHIP), assuming 30 employees with an average of two children qualify.

- $9,750 a year for the additional costs for low income energy assistance.

Among Wal-Mart employees, some single workers may be able to make ends meet. Others may be forced to take on two or three jobs. Others may have a spouse with a better job. And others simply cannot make ends meet. Because Wal-Mart fails to pay sufficient wages, U.S. taxpayers are forced to pick up the tab. In this sense, Wal-Mart's profits are not made only on the backs of its employees—but on the backs of every U.S. taxpayer....

Short-Sighted Profit-Making Strategies

Wal-Mart's success has meant downward pressures on wages and benefits, rampant violations of basic workers' rights, and threats to the standard of living in communities across the country. The success of a business need not come at the expense of workers and their families. Such short-sighted profit-making strategies ultimately undermine our economy. . . .

Wal-Mart's current behavior must not be allowed to set the standard for American labor practices. Standing together, America's working families, including Wal-Mart employees, and their allies in Congress can reverse this race to the bottom in the fast-expanding service industry. The promise that every American can work an honest day's work, receive an honest day's wages, raise a family, own a home, have decent health care, and send their children to college is a promise that is not easily abandoned. It is, in short, the American Dream.

> "The [television] industry could do more
> than pay lip service or promise time
> delays to clean up its own mess."

Television Networks Are Responsible for Offensive TV Shows

Dan K. Thomasson

Dan K. Thomasson, a retired investigative journalist and editor, worked for the Scripps Howard News Service in Washington, D.C., from the mid-1960s until 1998. In the following viewpoint Thomasson argues that the television broadcast media should regulate the content of their TV programs or risk having tighter regulations imposed on them by the federal government. In Thomasson's view, the networks have lowered their broadcast standards in an attempt to compete with cable programs, which he says are often obscene.

As you read, consider the following questions:

1. What risks does Thomasson indicate could come from the television industry's failure to regulate itself?

2. What complaint does the author lodge against reality programs such as *Survivor* ?

3. What does Thomasson think might be the only way to get media companies to offer decent programming?

M any years ago, an old friend predicted that television ultimately would become a series of situation comedies or dramas staged around the bedroom or bathroom and sponsored by the manufacturers of feminine-hygiene products or medicine for the treatment of hemorrhoids. He said the application of each product would be demonstrated live at least once during each broadcast.

Anyone paying attention to television, both free and pay, realizes full well that while it hasn't exactly reached that point of offensiveness, it is coming pretty close. So much so, in fact, that the issue of television sleaze and the Federal Communications Commission's [FCC] apparent inability to deal with it has become a major controversy once again. But this time the stakes could be high for everyone given the potential for censorship that lurks in every lawmaker.

The Problem

[Janet Jackson's] bare breast and suggestive gyrations in the midst of what was supposed to be wholesome entertainment called the [2004] Super Bowl is merely the catalyst for increasing public demands for some sort of regulation over the content of broadcast television. Janet Jackson's shocker or Madonna and Britney Spears kissing open-mouthed or Diane Keaton's four-letter exclamation of surprise during prime-time awards ceremonies are just the latest evidence that when it comes to taste, television's is limited to the endless daily recipes being inflicted on an overweight nation.

If the FCC—already under attack for rules that permit big media companies to own more and more stations, thereby further diluting local influence over programming—doesn't try to control the situation somehow, Congress is sure to do so. Given the political sensitivity to religious groups during an election year [2004], the results could be devastating to free expression, artistic and otherwise. Both the House and Senate

Proposals to Curb Indecency

—— Percent Who Favor Each Measure ——

	Govt. enforced family hour %	Increase fines %	Simple rating system %	Apply network rules to cable %
Total	75	69	61	60
Men	71	63	59	52
Women	79	75	63	68
Parent	78	71	63	56
Non-parent	74	69	60	62
Whites	77	71	64	60
Blacks	69	59	52	60
Hispanics	70	68	50	54
18–29	71	58	52	55
30–49	77	69	61	51
50–64	75	73	66	65
65+	78	79	67	79
Conserv Reps	84	83	72	71
Mod/Lib Reps	84	74	65	55
Independents	73	66	57	55
Cons/Mod Dems	79	74	62	65
Liberal Dems	52	47	55	46
White Protestants	84	79	68	68
–Evangelicals	89	87	67	80
–Non-Evangelicals	79	71	68	56
White Catholics	80	70	60	65
Seculars	53	46	47	36
Issue discussed in church?				
Yes	83	84	65	76
No	76	72	65	64

SOURCE: The Pew Research Center, "New Concerns About Internet and Reality Shows," April 19, 2005. www.people-press.org.

already have undertaken hearings on broadcast content and the FCC's approach to regulating it. Legislation has been introduced to increase to $275,000 the amount of fines that could be levied against networks for indecency and, understanding the dynamics here, that amount could go much higher.[1]

The Solution

There is an obvious preferable solution. The industry could do more than pay lip service or promise time delays to clean up its own mess, one that has been made worse by the popularity of trash talk on radio from scatological disc jockeys and trash video on television, from Jerry Springer to the spate of exploitation dramas produced under the "reality" label. The bachelor shows, males and females on the prowl, are particularly demeaning to both sexes, trivializing romance in a meat-market atmosphere.

Even the hugely successful "Survivor" series, which sparked it all, can't resist titillating its audience with scantily clad women participants, hints of sexual liaisons and even some jerk who insists on disrobing entirely during the show's silly challenges, much to the dismay of some of his fellow contestants who were visibly uncomfortable with his display. Viewers who stayed with CBS after the [2004] Super Bowl were treated to this guy's bare backside and blurred frontal nudity on numerous occasions.

Why, it seems fair to ask, didn't the network demand that he keep on his bathing suit or leave the show? It would have been a good first step toward convincing the public that it is serious about bringing some sense of decorum back to the medium. The answer seems to lie in the desperate efforts to compete with subscriber television, which has no restrictions and is cutting heavily into the audience share of traditional TV and ultimately its revenues. So what is now being sold to that portion of the public still committed to the non-pay vari-

1. Although both the House and the Senate passed versions of the bill, a compromise was not reached between the two houses on a final version, and the bill was never signed into law. A similar proposal was under consideration in 2005.

ety skirts closer and closer to the edge of what was once unthinkable in polite society.

None of this is surprising in a modern era of violence, sex and the depiction of nearly every sordid subject known to mankind. Huge dollars flow from this sensationalism, after all. But there are still many Americans who just don't want it piped into their front rooms while trying to watch what was a heck of a great football game or any other entertainment billed as for the entire family.

Perhaps the only way to get the message across is to hit the media companies where it hurts the most, in their wallets.

Unfortunately, that becomes a form of censorship that could carry into legitimate programs. It would be far better for the major players to censor themselves.

> "Ultimately, the solution to offensive
> programming lies not with policymak-
> ers but with individual consumers and
> families. . . . [The] most powerful
> weapons consumers wield are their
> own remote controls."

Consumers Are Responsible for Offensive TV Shows

James L. Gattuso

*James L. Gattuso is a specialist in regulatory and communica-
tions issues and serves as a research fellow in regulatory policy at
the Heritage Foundation's Roe Institute for Economic Policy
Studies. In the following viewpoint he grants that television programming is offensive, but he disagrees with those who want the
government to regulate TV indecency. Gattuso finds the regulatory approach to the issue problematic because it is difficult to
determine what constitutes obscenity. Instead, Gattuso proposes
that consumers simply stop watching offensive TV shows until
the television broadcast media begin producing more ethical content.*

As you read, consider the following questions:

1. As related by the author, what events and trends have
   led to a call for government regulation of broadcast
   media?

James L. Gattuso, "Broadcast Indecency: More Regulation Not the Answer," *WebMemo*,
February 15, 2005. Copyright © 2005 by The Heritage Foundation. Reproduced by permission.

2. What flaws does Gattuso find in the regulatory approach to curbing indecency in broadcast media?

3. What policies does Gattuso favor rather than stricter limits on media content?

T he halftime show at the Super Bowl game earlier this month [February 2005] went off without a hitch. Despite the nervous fears of network executives, there was no replay of the Janet Jackson "wardrobe malfunction" that shocked so many viewers last year.[1] Nevertheless, the nationwide debate over on-air indecency continued unabated: two days after the Super Bowl, the House Commerce Committee overwhelmingly approved legislation enhancing penalties for broadcast indecency. A vote by the full House is expected soon.[2]

Lawmakers are responding to a genuine concern, shared by many Americans, that television and radio broadcasts are becoming more offensive. However, the proposed solution, increased government restrictions on speech, is fundamentally misguided. Conservatives—who have long been the targets of politically correct speech codes on college campuses and elsewhere—should be particularly wary of this approach.

In the year since the Super Bowl shocker, the Federal Communications Commission (FCC) has undertaken a well-publicized campaign against indecency on the airwaves. For Jackson's revealing performance, the Commission slapped 20 stations owned by CBS with fines totaling $550,000. Last October [2004], the FCC fined 169 Fox Broadcasting affiliates a whopping $1.2 million, in total, for certain scenes on its short-lived "Married by America" show. In November, Viacom agreed to a $3.5 million settlement with the FCC for a number of broadcasts by radio "shock jocks."

The House legislation, H.R. 310, sponsored by Rep. Fred Upton [Rep.-Mich.], would raise the maximum fine for inde-

1. During the half-time entertainment, the singer's breast was exposed.

2. Neither the House legislation (H.R. 310) nor the Senate bill (S. 193) had been enacted as of November 2005.

cent broadcasts to as much as $500,000 per violation. (The limit under FCC guidelines today is $32,500.) It also would expand the FCC's authority to fine individuals responsible for on-air indecency, regardless of whether they hold licenses; allow the FCC to require broadcasters to air "educational" and "informational" programming (presumably approved by regulators) as a penalty for violations; and require the FCC to begin license revocation proceedings when a broadcaster has been fined three times or more.H.R. 310 is expected to move quickly to the full House of Representatives for a final vote. (The House approved similar legislation in 2004.)

Indecency legislation is also pending in the Senate: S. 193, sponsored by Sam Brownback [Rep.-Kansas], would increase per-incident fines to $325,000, with a maximum fine for indecency of $3,000,000.

Such proposals have broad support in Congress. Millions of Americans were outraged by the Janet Jackson incident, and lawmakers are looking for some way to express their own concern about diminishing standards of propriety on radio and television. And of course, no politician wants to be seen as soft on indecency.

The Problem

Considered more carefully, however, this regulatory approach is flawed and perhaps even dangerous. "Indecency" is a notoriously hard term to define. Content need not be obscene to be indecent, but it must be more than merely offensive or inappropriate. The FCC defines indecency as "language or material that, in context, depicts or describes, in terms patently offensive as measured by contemporary community standards for the broadcast medium, sexual or excretory organs or activities." This definition is as clear as mud.

In practice, the FCC determines whether particular content is indecent on a case-by-case basis. In the Super Bowl case, Janet Jackson's nudity made the cut. But what about the Monday Night Football ad for Fox's "Desperate Housewives" program, in which a woman dropped her towel to reveal her bare back, implying more than actually shown? Certain obscene words would seem clearly off-limits. But does it depend on context? Recently, a number of TV stations refused to show the movie *Saving Private Ryan* for fear that the FCC would take action due to the language used in the film. The FCC even received complaints about nudity during the opening of the Olympic games in Athens.

These fears may seem far-fetched but are very real to broadcasters who want to avoid fines and stand to lose their licenses. The chilling effect that results is very real, keeping much non-offensive—and valuable—material off the air.

Even more dangerously, the push for restrictions on indecency will, almost inevitably, lead to calls for restrictions on other types of content. Who could, for instance, oppose restrictions on "hate speech"—as, of course, defined by regulators. And what about content deemed "insensitive" to others in society? The path to politically correct speech codes is a clear one. Even controls on political speech are possible. There is already talk of re-imposing the "fairness doctrine," which required broadcasters to air both sides of controversial issues. The doctrine's effect was to discourage controversial issue-oriented programming. It was not until this rule was repealed in the 1980s that talk show hosts like Rush Limbaugh found a place on the radio dial.

The good—or bad—news is that any restrictions are likely to be ineffective. The FCC's restrictions apply only to television and radio stations that have licenses to broadcast over the airwaves. They do not apply, however, to TV or radio signals transmitted via cable or satellite. This means a majority of television programming and—with the advent of satellite radio—an increasing share of radio programming is out of regulators' reach. Increased broadcast restrictions would only accelerate the growth of these non-controlled media at the ex-

FCC Indecency Guidelines

Indecency findings involve at least two fundamental determinations. First, the material alleged to be indecent must fall within the subject matter scope of our indecency definition—that is, the material must describe or depict sexual or excretory organs or activities.

Second, the broadcast must be *patently offensive* as measured by contemporary community standards for the broadcast medium. In applying the "community standards for the broadcast medium" criterion, the Commission has stated:

> The determination as to whether certain programming is patently offensive is not a local one and does not encompass any particular geographic area. Rather, the standard is that of an average broadcast viewer or listener and not the sensibilities of any individual complainant.

In determining whether material is patently offensive, the *full context* in which the material appeared is critically important. It is not sufficient, for example, to know that explicit sexual terms or descriptions were used, just as it is not sufficient to know only that no such terms or descriptions were used. Explicit language in the context of a *bona fide* newscast might not be patently offensive, while sexual innuendo that persists and is sufficiently clear to make the sexual meaning inescapable might be. Moreover, contextual determinations are necessarily highly fact-specific, making it difficult to catalog comprehensively all of the possible contextual factors that might exacerbate or mitigate the patent offensiveness of particular material.

Federal Communications Commission,
Policy Statement, April 6, 2001.

pense of the regulated ones: witness, for example, Howard Stern's jump to the Sirius satellite radio network.

Recognizing this, some propose extending the FCC's rules to non-broadcast media. But such a move would almost certainly be unconstitutional. The current rules are made possible only by the presumed scarcity of broadcast frequencies, which courts have ruled justifies more extensive government involvement in content that otherwise would be allowed. Cable and satellite providers face no such scarcity. And if these providers *were* to be regulated, why wouldn't traditional print media such as newspapers and magazines be vulnerable, as well? What about the Internet, over which audio and video are already "broadcast" today? Such comprehensive government control of the media would likely be too much for the courts—or even lawmakers—to contemplate.

The Solution

Rather than impose ever-stricter limits on media content, lawmakers concerned about the quality of programming should instead promote policies that would expand the choices available to consumers. Already, cable programmers such as the Family Channel and Disney Channel offer family-oriented television. Many more are available on satellite television. And Sirius—despite its Howard Stern deal—announced it would offer several channels of children's radio on its satellite network.

By reducing governmental barriers to new outlets, policymakers could further increase the number of choices available. Such steps could include freeing up underused radio spectrum, reducing regulations that discourage investment in new telecommunications systems, and reducing taxes on providers.

Ultimately, the solution to offensive programming lies not with policymakers but with individual consumers and families. Parents and others unhappy with what they see on the television have available to them weapons more powerful than has any congressman. Like other businesses, broadcasters respond to their customers. Complaints to broadcasters and to the advertisers that support them can be effective. But the most powerful weapons consumers wield are their own remote controls. As conservatives know well, the best regulation comes not from government but from individuals making choices for themselves. Rather than look to Washington for answers, we should look to our own thumbs.

"The disdain that so many [liberal] reporters have for the military (or for police, the FBI, conservative Christians, or right-to-lifers) frames the way that errors and bogus stories tend to occur."

The Liberal Media Distort the News

John Leo

In the following viewpoint John Leo claims that there is an overarching liberal prejudice amongst American journalists. According to Leo, such bias exists in the media because there is little intellectual diversity among journalists, who often share a similar economic and liberal educational background. Finally, he asserts, the mainstream media is losing credibility with the public and faces an uncertain future. A columnist with U.S. News & World Report, *Leo has contributed to such periodicals as* Time, *Commonweal, the* Village Voice, *and the* New York Times.

As you read, consider the following questions:

1. To what does Leo attribute the perceived anti-military bias in the media?

2. In Leo's view, what is the biggest flaw in mainstream journalism?

3. Why does Leo believe that the press must change or
lose its audience?

It's official. Conservatives are losing their monopoly on
complaints about media bias. In the wake of *Newsweek*'s
bungled report that U.S. military interrogators "flushed a
Qur'an down a toilet [at a U.S. military prison in Guántanmo
Bay, Cuba]," here is Terry Moran, ABC's White House reporter, in an interview with radio host and blogger Hugh
Hewitt: "There is, I agree with you, a deep antimilitary bias in
the media, one that begins from the premise that the military
must be lying and that American projection of power around
the world must be wrong." Moran thinks it's a hangover from
Vietnam. Sure, but the culture of the newsroom is a factor,
too. In all my years in journalism, I don't think I have met
more than one or two reporters who have ever served in the
military or who even had a friend in the armed forces. Most
media hiring today is from universities where a military career
is regarded as bizarre and almost any exercise of American
power is considered wrongheaded or evil.

Not long ago, memorable comments about press credibility came from two stars at *Newsweek*: Evan Thomas and
Howard Fineman. During the [2004] presidential campaign,
Thomas said on TV that the news media wanted John Kerry
to win. We knew that, but the candor was refreshing. Fineman
said during the flap over Dan Rather and CBS's use of forged
documents on the George Bush-National Guard story: "A political party is dying before our eyes—and I don't mean the
Democrats. I'm talking about the 'mainstream media.' ... It's
hard to know now who, if anyone, in the 'media' has any credibility." It's worth mentioning here that the unrepentant Rather
and his colleague Mary Mapes, who was fired for her role in
presenting the forged documents, received a major industry
award ..., a Peabody, as well as "extended applause" from the

Journalism Is an Act of Character

Since there are no laws of journalism, no regulations, no licensing, and no formal self-policing, and since journalism by its nature can be exploitative, a heavy burden rests on the ethics and judgment of the individual journalist and the individual organization where he or she works. . . .

Whether or not we are conscious of the importance of this characteristic, when all is said and done what we are choosing when we select a magazine, a TV program, a website, or a paper is the authority, honesty, and judgment of the journalists who produce it.

As a consequence, there is a final principle that journalists have come to understand about their work and that we as citizens intuit when we make our media choices. It is the most elusive of the principles, yet it ties all the others together:

Journalists have an obligation to personal conscience.

Every journalist—from the newsroom to the boardroom—must have a personal sense of ethics and responsibility—a moral compass. What's more, they have a responsibility to voice their personal conscience out loud and allow others around them to do so as well. . . .

Simply put, those who inhabit news organizations must recognize a personal obligation to differ with or challenge editors, owners, advertisers, and even citizens and established authority if fairness and accuracy require they do so.

Bill Kovach and Tom Rosenstiel,
The Elements of Journalism, *2001.*

journalists in the crowd. (What's next? A lifetime achievement award for *New York Times* prevaricator Jayson Blair?)

Bias-Prone

Instead of trampling *Newsweek*—the magazine made a mistake and corrected it quickly and honestly—the focus ought to be on whether the news media are predisposed to make certain kinds of mistakes and, if so, what to do about it. The disdain that so many reporters have for the military (or for police, the FBI, conservative Christians, or right-to-lifers) frames the way that errors and bogus stories tend to occur. The antimilitary mentality makes atrocity stories easier to publish, even when they are untrue. The classic example is CNN's false 1998 story that the U.S. military knowingly dropped nerve gas on Americans during the Vietnam War. On the other hand, brutal treatment of dissenters by Fidel Castro tends to be softened or omitted in the American press because so many journalists still see him as the romanticized figure from their youth in the 1960s. Another example: It's possible to read newspapers and newsmagazines carefully and never see anything about the liberal indoctrination now taking place at major universities. This has something to do with the fact that the universities are mostly institutions of the left and that newsrooms tend to hire from the left and from the universities in question.

I once complained to an important news executive that he ignored certain kinds of stories. He said that he would like to do them but that his staff wouldn't let him. He admitted his staff had been assembled from one side—guess which?—of the political spectrum. This conversation hardened my conviction that the biggest flaw in mainstream journalism today is the lack of diversity. Much bean-counting goes on in regard to gender and race, but the new hires tend to come from the same economic bracket and the same pool of elite universities, and they tend to have the same take on politics and culture. Much of what they turn out is very good. But when they omit or mess up stories, run badly skewed polls, or publish front-page editorials posing as news stories, nobody seems to notice because groupthink is so strong.

Time is running out on the newsroom monoculture. The public has many options now—as well as plenty of media watchdogs, both professional and amateur. So the press takes its lumps and loses readers. In March [2005], a report on the state of the media by the Project for Excellence in Journalism said that in the past 17 years, Americans have "come to see the press as less professional, less moral, more inaccurate, and less caring about the interests of the country." According to the report, fewer than half of Americans think of the press as highly professional (49 percent, down from 72 percent 17 years ago). Another finding was that coverage of George Bush during the presidential campaign was three times as negative as coverage of John Kerry (36 percent to 12 percent). If the press is that much out of sync with the country, its future looks very uncertain. Something has to change.

> "What all ... examples [of 'liberal bias' in the media] have in common is the absence of evidence for their accusations."

The Media Does Not Have a Liberal Bias

Eric Alterman

Eric Alterman is a media critic, columnist, and author of several political studies, including What Liberal Media? The Truth About Bias and the News. *In the following viewpoint he disputes claims by conservative commentators that the* New York Times *and other major newspapers are liberal publications. Rather, according to Alterman, many publications have become hostile to liberals in an effort to placate conservatives. Alterman asserts that those who claim that the media has a liberal bias never have evidence to prove their case.*

As you read, consider the following questions:

1. In Alterman's view, what offsets the fact that most employees of the *New York Times* are social liberals?

2. What steps did the *New York Times* management take in an effort to appeal to conservative readers, according to the author?

3. How does Alterman counter the conservative accusation that liberals are the "biggest risk" to U.S. policy in Iraq?

To anyone paying attention, it ought to be obvious that the conservative caricature of the *New York Times* as a hotbed of liberal agitation is just too good to be true. Even though employees of the *Times*, like most urban professionals, are likely social liberals, this is offset by their commitment to objectivity and professionalism, coupled with a similar—though largely unremarked-upon—class bias toward a relatively conservative, business-friendly outlook on economic issues. (Wishing to offer advertisers a friendly environment does not lead in the direction of economic populism either.) Add to this its reporters' and editors' establishment-bred inability to disbelieve Bush Administration lies, no matter how frequently or brazenly offered, and the *Times* news pages frequently end up tilting rightward.

What lies behind the right-wing attacks, aside from a certain fanaticism among the assailants, is what *Weekly Standard* senior writer Matt Labash termed the right's "cottage industry" or "great little racket," in which "the conservative media like to rap the liberal media on the knuckles for not being objective. . . . It's a great way to have your cake and eat it, too."

Under relentless pressure from the [conservative Rush] Limbaughs, [Bill] O'Reillys and [Joe] Scarboroughs of the world—as well as the right-wing blogosphere, the [Rupert] Murdoch empire, the Republican National Committee, etc.— the machers who run the *Times* are concerned that their brand of reality-based reporting is increasingly out of step with faith-based red [conservative] America. Op-ed columnist Nicholas Kristof wrote that the paper suffers from a "failure to hire more red state evangelicals." A recent "credibility" committee formed in the wake of the Blair and WMD scandals[1] somehow resulted in a meeting, written up by Todd Gitlin in *The American Prospect,* in which one editor suggested an affirmative-action program for conservatives. And following the committee's report, executive editor Bill Keller sent the staff a memo urging reporters and editors to "stretch beyond our predominantly urban, culturally liberal orientation."

Even before the committee was convened, however, some reporters and editors had started taking matters into their own hands. But instead of "stretching" toward conservatives, they started stabbing at liberals—launching a fusillade of furious (and largely gratuitous) attacks on these apparently alien creatures. It's almost as if a secret *Times* directive had agreed to release reporters from typical standards of evidence if it would help to shake the paper's dreaded "liberal" label. Some examples:

On the news pages, then-political reporter now op-ed columnist John Tierney told of stationing himself outside the storied Upper West Side food store Zabar's during the GOP [Republican Party] convention to ask shoppers—presumably liberal by location—if they had "re-examined their conscience" (for what, he did not explain).

In the magazine, Michael Ignatieff complained of "the withdrawal of American liberalism from the defense and promotion of freedom overseas," as well as the alleged conquest of "the Democratic Party's heart" by "the [documentary maker] Michael Moore-style left."

In the [*Times's*] Book Review [section], *Slate* editor Jacob Weisberg complained that author Graydon Carter offered a "free pass" to "Michael Moore, Joe Conason, Eric Alterman, Sidney Blumenthal," which "calls into question his choice of targets like Thomas Friedman, Andrew Sullivan and my col-

1. Documents were made public in 2005 that implicated Prime Minister Tony Blair and other British government officials in a plan to fit intelligence and facts regarding Iraq's possession of weapons of mass destruction (WMD) into an already-established U.S. policy for the forceful removal of Saddam Hussein from power.

Conservative Control of the Media

The Republicans ... have a huge structural advantage. They can spend far more money getting their message out; when it comes to free publicity, some of the major broadcast media are simply biased in favor of the Republicans, while the rest tend to blur differences between the parties.

But that's the way it is. Democrats should complain as loudly about the real conservative bias of the media as the Republicans complain about its entirely mythical liberal bias; that will help them get their substantive message across.

Paul Krugman, New York Times, *November 8, 2002.*

league Mickey Kaus, shrewder commentators with whom he simply disagrees." Weisberg's review also deemed MSNBC's prewar cancellation of Phil Donahue's liberal talk show—its highest-rated program at the time—a matter of economics, not politics, despite well-publicized internal NBC memos indicating otherwise.

On the op-ed page, Thomas Friedman, sounding like a mind-reading Joe McCarthy, explained, "Liberals don't want to talk about Iraq because ... deep down [they] don't want the Bush team to succeed."

In one op-ed column Nicholas Kristof explained, "These days, the biggest risk may come from the small but growing contingent on the left that wants to bring our troops home now." In another, he complained of the "liberal tendency in America to blame ourselves for Africa's problems."

In a forthcoming Book Review essay, conservative jurist Richard Posner spends more than 4,600 words beating the antiliberal drum (again attacking yours truly).

What all these examples have in common is the absence of evidence for their accusations, much less a response from those under attack. Friedman, for instance, comes pretty close to accusing liberals of rooting for the enemy yet can't be bothered to name a single person to whom this heinous charge applies. Ditto Kristof. Did he lack space to name one liberal who blames America for Africa's woes? And why were Weisberg's more conservative writers so much "shrewder" than we liberals? Moreover, just what do the publications of three careful journalists, who write heavily footnoted works of reporting and scholarship, have do to with the entertaining agit-prop of Michael Moore? In the words of [TV classic *I Love Lucy's*] Ricky Ricardo, "Splain, please." Meanwhile, Posner bases his argument on inaccurate data and discredited works by the likes of Bernard Goldberg and L. Brent Bozell, never once defining what he means by "liberal newspaper or television news channel."

Some of these charges are almost comical. How could it possibly be, *pace* Kristof, that liberals are the "biggest risk" to US policy in Iraq or indeed to anything, anywhere? We don't even control *The New Republic* anymore, much less Bush's National Security Council, the Pentagon or the CIA. Tierney described the Upper West Side as "the neighborhood that has called itself 'the conscience of the nation.'" This is not only false but theoretically impossible. Neighborhoods do not call themselves anything. They lack the power of speech, for starters.

So why do such baseless attacks on liberals make it through the *Times* editorial process? Did we put [journalist] Jayson Blair's fictions on the front page? Did we instruct [journalist] Judith Miller to channel [vice president Dick] Cheney and [Iraqi official Ahmed] Chalabi in her WMD reporting? As a liberal, I have no doubt we're guilty . . . of *something*.

Periodical Bibliography

The following articles have been selected to supplement the diverse views presented in this chapter.

Ken Auletta	"Backstory: Inside the Business of News," Carnegie Council on Ethics and International Affairs, January 14, 2004. www.carnegiecouncil-.org.
Matthew T. Felling	"Media Makeovers: 'Michelibs' Left off the Airwaves?" *San Francisco Chronicle*, November 2, 2003.
Bruce Frohnen and Leo Clarke	"Scandal in Corporate America: An Ethical, Not a Legal, Problem," *USA Today*, November 1, 2002.
Anthony Harrington	"In Good Company," *Financial Director*, July 4, 2005.
Richard Hudson	"Ethical Investing: Ethical Investors and Managers," *Business Ethics Quarterly*, October 2005.
Kevin T. Jackson	"Towards Authenticity: A Sartrean Perspective on Business Ethics," *Journal of Business Ethics*, June 2005.
Jeffrey Marshall	"Corporate Social Responsibility: Hard Choices on Soft Issues," *Financial Executive*, July/August 2005.
James Poniewozik	"The Decency Police," *Time*, March 28, 2005.
Joe Sibilia	"In Business, Social Goals Also Matter," *PR Week*, October 24, 2005.
Amy Sullivan	"The Biases Are Loaded," *American Prospect Online*, April 28, 2003, www.prospect.org.
Cathy Young	"Media Critic, Critique Thyself," *Reason Online*, July 2003. www.reason.com.

For Further Discussion

Chapter 1

1. The foundation of ethics is understood by Lewis B. Smedes to be in spiritual beliefs, by Donald W. Murphy to be in physical responses, and by Gregory D. Foster to be in intellectual processes. While each writer begins from a different perspective, what similarities emerge in their arguments about the motivation to behave ethically?

2. According to Randy Cohen, most people simply look at how others act to determine the right behavior when faced with an ethical decision. How does this viewpoint correspond or contrast with the ideas of the other authors in this chapter?

3. Steve Johnson believes that students can and should be taught ethics in school. Do you agree that schools have a responsibility to teach values to children? Explain why or why not.

Chapter 2

1. John McConnell establishes preservation of the earth as the primary aim of ethical behavior, and Federico Mayor Zaragoza believes that solidarity with future generations ought to guide the behavior of those now alive. Which traditional values would you say underlie these positions?

2. Catholic theologian Sidney Callahan asserts that "ethics is an art, not a science." Do you agree or disagree with that perception? Explain.

3 Lawrence Kelemen maintains that parents often do not live up to the standards they espouse for their children, and Stuart C. Gilman argues that providing a list of rules for officials is insufficient to guide the behavior of government

officials. Discuss the ways in which you believe these authors would agree or disagree regarding the effectiveness of codes of behavior.

Chapter 3

1. The ethical debates surrounding assisted reproductive technologies (ART), embryonic stem cell research, and cloning center on defining what it means to be *human* and what it means to be a *person*. For some authors, such as Michael D. West and Gregory Stock, the moral responsibility to seek medical advances to benefit people outweighs all other considerations. Others, such as M. D. Harmon and Brian Caulfield, believe that each human being is sacred and unique, and that research that destroys life or that replicates it is therefore unethical regardless of the possible benefits. In your opinion, what does it mean to be *human* ? What does it mean to be a *person* ? Are human beings, at whatever stage of development, appropriate subjects for scientific experimentation? Explain.

2. John Shelby Spong argues that a belief in the sacredness of human life is best reflected in the choice to end life when it becomes severely compromised by disease or suffering. Edward J. Richard contends that belief in the sacredness of human life ought to prevent innocent human beings from being killed by any act or omission, even if done to relieve suffering. Who do you think makes the stronger argument? Explain your answer.

Chapter 4

1. Andrew E. Reisman maintains that by focusing on ethics, businesses will reap financial rewards. The *Economist* holds that the aim of business is profit, and that social good will follow from success. A case in American business is Wal-Mart. Its detractors, including author George Miller, criticize Wal-Mart for focusing on profitability rather than on

the welfare of its employees and their communities. However, defenders such as Karen De Coster contend that Wal-Mart does nothing wrong to give American shoppers what they want: convenience, quality, selection, and low prices. In your opinion, what motivation do businesses have for focusing on social issues before profit? How can a business prioritize the often-conflicting responsibilities they have to their employees, their shareholders, their suppliers, their customers, and the community?

2. James L. Gattuso argues that television network programming is often offensive but that the government should not impose regulations mandating decency; the proper response, he says, is for consumers to refuse to watch offensive programming. Dan K. Thomasson, on the other hand, believes that if television networks do not begin regulating programming content then the government should intervene to impose decency standards. From your own experience, do you believe television programming is offensive or indecent? Do you agree or disagree with arguments favoring government regulation? Explain.

3. John Leo claims that there is an overarching liberal prejudice among American journalists. Eric Alterman perceives a conservative bias in news reporting. Who do you think makes the stronger case for bias? Is unbiased journalism even possible? Explain your answers.

Organizations to Contact

Accuracy in the Media
4455 Connecticut Ave. NW, Suite 330
  Washington, DC 20008
(202) 364-4401 • fax: (202) 364-4098
Web site: www.aim.org

Accuracy in the Media is a conservative watchdog organization. It researches public complaints on errors of fact made by the news media and requests that the errors be corrected publicly. It publishes the bimonthly *AIM Report* and a weekly syndicated newspaper column.

American Family Association (AFA)
PO Drawer 2440, Tupelo, MS 38803
(662) 844-5036 • fax: (662) 842-7798

The American Family Association (formerly the National Federation for Decency) works to improve the morality of America. The AFA opposes what it sees as the proliferation of violence, profanity, vulgarity, and pornography in popular entertainment. It sponsors letter-writing campaigns to encourage television sponsors to support only quality programming, and it compiles statistics on how media violence affects society. The association's publications include books, videos, the monthly *AFA Journal*, and the *AFA Action Alert* newsletter.

American Society of Law, Medicine, and Ethics (ASLME)
765 Commonwealth Ave., Suite 1634
  Boston, MA 02215
(617) 262-4990 • fax: (617) 437-7596
Web site: www.aslme.org

The members of the American Society of Law, Medicine, and Ethics include physicians, attorneys, health care administrators, and others interested in the relationship between law, medicine, and ethics. ASLME takes no positions but acts as a forum for discussion of issues such as genetic engineering. The organization has an information clearinghouse and a library. It publishes the quarterlies *American Journal of Law & Medicine* and the *Journal of Law, Medicine & Ethics*; the periodic *ASLME Briefings*; and various books.

Association for Practical and Professional Ethics (APPE)
Indiana University
   Bloomington, IN 47405-3602
(812) 855-6450 • fax: (812) 855-3315
Web site: www.indiana.edu

The Association for Practical and Professional Ethics (APPE) encourages interdisciplinary scholarship and teaching in practical and professional ethics. The APPE facilitates joint ventures among centers, schools, colleges, businesses, nonprofit organizations, and individuals concerned with the interdisciplinary study and teaching of practical and professional ethics. APPE publishes the *Practical and Professional Ethics* series in cooperation with Oxford University Press. APPE also publishes the newsletter *Ethically Speaking*, the six-volume series *Research Ethics: Cases and Commentaries*, and such handbooks and monographs as *How to Survive Graduate School and Start Your Career in Science/Engineering* and *Ethics Centers and Conflict of Interest*.

Canadian Centre for Ethics and Corporate Policy
One Yonge St., Suite 1801
   Toronto ON M5E 1W7 Canada
(416) 368-7525 • fax: (416) 369-0515
Web site: www.ethicscentre.ca

The Canadian Centre for Ethics and Corporate Policy includes corporations and individuals dedicated to developing and maintaining an ethical corporate culture. It supports research into issues concerning corporate ethics and sponsors seminars, conferences, and lectures on business ethics. It publishes the bimonthly newsletter *Management Ethics*.

Center for Applied Christian Ethics
Wheaton College, Wheaton, IL 60187-5593
(630) 752-5886 • fax: (630) 752-5731
Web site: www.christianethics.org

The goal of the Center for Applied Christian Ethics is to raise moral awareness and elicit moral thinking by encouraging the application of Christian ethics to public policy and personal practice. The center sponsors conferences, workshops, and public debates on ethical issues. It produces a variety of resource materials, including cassettes, videotapes, the newsletter *Discernment*, and the booklet "The Bible, Ethics, and Health Care: Theological Foundations for a Christian Perspective on Health Care."

Center for Bioethics
University of Pennsylvania
  Philadelphia, PA 19104
(215) 898-7136
Web site: www.bioethics.upenn.edu

The University of Pennsylvania's Center for Bioethics is the largest bioethics center of its kind in the world, and it runs the world's first and largest bioethics Web site. It engages in research and publishes articles about many areas of bioethics, including gene therapy and genetic engineering. The center publishes both the quarterly newsletter *PennBioethics* and the *American Journal of Bioethics*.

Center for Bioethics and Human Dignity
2065 Half Day Rd., Bannockburn, IL 60015
(847) 317-8180 • fax: (847) 317-8101
Web site: www.cbhd.org

The Center for Bioethics and Human Dignity is an international education center whose purpose is to bring Christian perspectives to bear on contemporary bioethical challenges facing society. Its publications address genetic technologies as well as other topics such as euthanasia and abortion. It publishes the newsletter *Dignity* and the book *Genetic Ethics: Do the Ends Justify the Genes?*

Center for Business Ethics (CBE)
Bentley College, Waltham, MA 02452-4705
(781) 891-2981 • fax: (781) 891-2988
Web site: http://ecampus.bentley.edu

The Center for Business Ethics is dedicated to promoting ethical business conduct in contemporary society. It helps corporations and other organizations strengthen their ethical cultures through educational programming and consulting. The center maintains a multimedia library and publishes the quarterly journal *Business and Society Review*. CBE also publishes a variety of books, including *Business Ethics: A Primer* and *Ethics Matters: How to Implement Values-Driven Management*.

Council for Secular Humanism
PO Box 664, Amherst, NY 14226-0664
(716) 636-7571 • fax: (716) 636-1733
Web site: www.secularhumanism.org

The Council for Secular Humanism is an educational organization dedicated to fostering the growth of democracy, secular humanism, and the principles of free inquiry. It publishes the magazine *Free Inquiry* as well as papers in the Secular Humanist Viewpoints series, such as "Are the Ten Commandments Relevant Today?"

Dying with Dignity
55 Eglinton Ave. E, Suite 802
   Toronto ON M4P 1G8 Canada
(416) 486-3998 • fax: (416) 486-5562
Web site: www.dyingwithdignity.ca

Dying with Dignity works to improve the quality of dying for all Canadians in accordance with their wishes, values, and beliefs. It educates Canadians about their right to choose health care options at the end of life, provides counseling and advocacy services to those who request them, and builds public support for voluntary physician-assisted dying. Dying with Dignity publishes a newsletter and maintains an extensive library of euthanasia-related materials.

Ethics Resource Center
1747 Pennsylvania Ave. NW, Suite 400
  Washington, DC 20006
(202) 737-2258
Web site: www.ethics.org

The Ethics Resource Center works to restore America's ethical foundations by fostering integrity, ethical conduct, and basic values in the nation's institutions. It also strives to create international coalitions dedicated to global ethics. The center supports character education and has developed several video-based learning programs for use in schools. Its publications include *Creating a Workable Company Code of Ethics, The Desktop Guide to Total Ethics Management,* and the quarterly newsletter *Ethics Today.*

Fairness and Accuracy in Reporting (FAIR)
112 W. Twenty-seventh St.
  New York, NY 10001
(212) 633-6700 • fax: (212) 727-7668
Web site: www.fair.org

FAIR is a national media watchdog group that offers documented criticism of media bias and censorship. It believes that the media are controlled by, and support, corporate and governmental interests and that they are insensitive to women, labor, minorities, and other special-interest groups. It publishes the bimonthly magazine *Extra!*

The Hastings Center
21 Malcolm Gordon Rd., Harrison, NY 10524-5555
(845) 424-4040 • fax: (845) 424-4545
www.thehastingscenter.org

Since its founding in 1969, the Hastings Center has played a central role in responding to developments in medicine, the biological sciences, and the social sciences by raising ethical questions related to such advances. It conducts research on ethical issues and provides consultations. The center publishes books, papers, guidelines, and the bimonthly *Hastings Center Report.*

Institute for Global Ethics
11 Main St., PO Box 563
  Camden, ME 04843
(207) 236-6658 • fax: (207) 236-4014
Web site: www.globalethics.org

Dedicated to fostering global ethics, the Institute for Global Ethics focuses on ethical activities in education, the corporate sector, and public policy. It conducts ethics training seminars, sponsors lectures and workshops, develops curricular materials for elementary and secondary schools, and promotes community-based character education programs. Its publications include the quarterly newsletter *Insights on Global Ethics* and the books *How Good People Make Tough Choices: Resolving the Dilemmas of Ethical Living* and *Heartland Ethics: Voices from the American Midwest.*

Josephson Institute of Ethics
9841 Airport Blvd., #300
  Los Angeles, CA 90045
(310) 846-4800 • fax: (310) 846-4857
Web site: www.josephsoninstitute.org

The Josephson Institute of Ethics is a nonprofit membership organization founded to improve the ethical quality of society by teaching and advocating principled reasoning and ethical decision making. Its Government Ethics Center has conducted programs and workshops for more than twenty thousand influential leaders. Its publications include the newsletter *Ethics in Action*, the quarterly *Ethics: Easier Said than Done*, and reports such as *Ethics of American Youth: A Warning and a Call to Action.*

Joseph and Rose Kennedy Institute of Ethics
Healy, Fourth Floor, Georgetown University
  Washington, DC 20057
(202) 687-8099 • fax: (202) 687-8089
Web site: www.georgetown.edu

Established at Georgetown University in 1971, the Kennedy Institute of Ethics is a teaching and research center that offers ethical perspectives on major policy issues, especially in the biomedical field. Issues related to human genetics and gene alteration are among the subjects it considers. The institute's publications include the quarterly journal *Kennedy Institute of Ethics Journal*, an annual bibliography, and an encyclopedia. It also produces a series of papers that present overviews of issues and viewpoints related to particular topics in biomedical ethics.

Markkula Center for Applied Ethics
500 El Camino Real
   Santa Clara, CA 95053
(408) 554-5319 • fax: (408) 554-2373
Web site: www.scu.edu

The Markkula Center for Applied Ethics at Santa Clara University addresses such issues as business, health care, biotechnology, character education, government, global leadership, technology, and emerging issues in ethics. The center does not advocate positions as an organization, but individuals within the center may make position statements. The center publishes the journal *Issues in Ethics* and makes articles, briefings, and other resources available on its Web site.

The Nuffield Council on Bioethics
28 Bedford Square
   London WC1B 3JS England
(020) 7681 9619 • fax: (020) 7637 1712
Web site: www.nuffieldbioethics.org

The Nuffield Council on Bioethics works to identify, examine, and report on the ethical questions raised by recent advances in biological and medical research. It also seeks to play a role in policy making and stimulating debate about bioethics. The council has published major reports on the ethical issues associated with such topics as genetic screening, ownership of tissue, xenotransplantation, genetics and mental disorders, stem cell therapy, DNA patenting, ethics in pharmacogenics, and genetics and human behavior.

President's Council on Bioethics
1801 Pennsylvania Ave. NW, Suite 700
  Washington, DC 20006
(202) 296-4669
Web site: www.bioethics.gov

When the National Bioethics Advisory Commission's charter expired in October 2001, President George W. Bush established the President's Council on Bioethics. It works to protect the rights and welfare of human research subjects and govern the management and use of genetic information. On its Web site the council provides access to its reports "Human Cloning and Human Dignity: An Ethical Inquiry" and "Beyond Therapy: Biotechnology and the Pursuit of Happiness."

Traditional Values Coalition (TVC)
139 C St. SE, Washington, DC 20003
(202) 547-8570 • fax: (202) 546-6403
Web site: www.traditionalvalues.org

The Traditional Values Coalition strives to restore what the group believes are the traditional moral and spiritual values in American government, schools, media, and society. It defines traditional values as "a moral code and behavior based upon the Old and New Testaments . . . the moral precepts taught by Jesus Christ and by the whole counsel of God as revealed in the Bible." TVC publishes the quarterly newsletter *Traditional Values Report* as well as various information papers.

Bibliography of Books

Eric Alterman

What Liberal Media? The Truth About Bias and the News. New York: Basic Books, 2003.

Kwame Anthony Appiah

Cosmopolitanism: Ethics in a World of Strangers. New York: W.W. Norton, 2006.

Anthony Bianco

The Bully of Bentonville: How the High Cost of Wal-Mart's Everyday Low Prices Is Hurting America. New York: Currency/Doubleday, 2006.

Michele Borba

Building Moral Intelligence: The Seven Essential Virtues That Teach Kids to Do the Right Thing. San Francisco: Jossey-Bass, 2001.

Michael C. Brannigan, ed.

Ethical Issues in Human Cloning: Cross-Disciplinary Perspectives. New York: Seven Bridges, 2001.

Donald M. Broom

The Evolution of Morality and Religion: A Biological Perspective. Cambridge, England: Cambridge University Press, 2004.

Robert Buckman

Can We Be Good Without God? Biology, Behavior, and the Need to Believe. Amherst, NY: Prometheus, 2002.

William Casebeer

Natural Ethical Facts: Evolution, Connectionism, and Moral Cognition. Cambridge, MA: MIT Press, 2003.

Joanne B. Ciulla, Clancy Martin, and Robert C. Solomon

Honest Work: A Business Ethics Reader. New York: Oxford University Press, 2006.

William Damon	*The Moral Advantage: How to Succeed in Business by Doing the Right Thing.* San Francisco: Berrett-Koehler, 2004.
David DeGrazia	*Human Identity and Bioethics.* New York: Cambridge University Press, 2005.
John Dicker	*The United States of Wal-Mart.* New York: Jeremy P. Tarcher/Penguin, 2005.
Robert H. Frank	*What Price the Moral High Ground? Ethical Dilemmas in Competitive Environments.* Princeton, NJ: Princeton University Press, 2004.
Robert P. George	*The Clash of Orthodoxies: Law, Religion, and Morality in Crisis.* Wilmington, DE: ISI Books, 2001.
Mark Gibney	*Five Uneasy Pieces: American Ethics in a Globalized World.* Lanham, MD: Rowman & Littlefield, 2005.
Scott F. Gilbert, Anna L. Tyler, and Emily J. Zackin	*Bioethics and the New Embryology: Springboards for Debate.* New York: W.H. Freeman, 2005.
Bernard Goldberg	*Bias: A CBS Insider Exposes How the Media Distorts the News.* Washington, DC: Regnery, 2001.
A. C. Grayling	*Meditations for the Humanist: Ethics for a Secular Age.* New York: Oxford University Press, 2002.
David E. Guinn, ed.	*Handbook of Bioethics and Religion.* New York: Oxford University Press, 2006.

Michael Ignatieff — *The Lesser Evil: Political Ethics in an Age of Terror.* Edinburgh, Scotland: Edinburgh University Press, 2005.

Mary Jo Iozzio, ed. — *Considering Religious Traditions in Bioethics: Christian and Jewish Voices.* Scranton, PA: University of Scranton Press, 2001.

Peter Michael Jack — *Thou Dust: A Philosophical Essay on Cloning.* Toronto: Timefoot Books, 2003.

John Keown — *Euthanasia, Ethics, and Public Policy: An Argument Against Legalization.* New York: Cambridge University Press, 2002.

Rushworth M. Kidder — *Moral Courage.* New York: William Morrow, 2005.

Paul Kurtz — *Humanist Manifesto 2000: A Call for a New Planetary Humanism.* Amherst, NY: Prometheus, 2000.

Paul Lauritzen, ed. — *Cloning and the Future of Human Embryo Research.* New York: Oxford University Press, 2001.

Daniel E. Lee — *Navigating Right and Wrong: Ethical Decision Making in a Pluralistic Age.* Lanham, MD: Rowman & Littlefield, 2002.

Carol W. Lewis and Stuart C. Gilman — *The Ethics Challenge in Public Service: A Problem-Solving Guide.* 2⁰ ed. San Francisco: Jossey-Bass, 2005.

Barry A. Liebling — *Think and Act on Business Ethics: A Radical Capitalist View.* New York: Alert Mind, 2004.

Alan Lightman, Daniel Sarewitz, and Christina Desser, eds.	*Living with the Genie: Essays on Technology and the Quest for Human Mastery.* Washington, DC: Island Press, 2003.
Barbara MacKinnon, ed.	*Human Cloning: Science, Ethics, and Public Policy.* Urbana: University of Illinois Press, 2000.
Michael Martin	*Atheism, Morality, and Meaning.* Amherst, NY: Prometheus, 2002.
John C. Maxwell	*There's No Such Thing as "Business" Ethics: There's Only One Rule for Making Decisions.* New York: Warner Books, 2003.
Glenn McGee nd Arthur Caplan, eds.	*Human Cloning Debate.* 4th ed. Berkeley, CA: Berkeley Hills Books, 2004.
Quinn McKay	*The Bottom Line on Integrity: 12 Principles for Higher Returns.* Layton, UT: Gibbs Smith, 2004.
Asher Meir	*The Jewish Ethicist: Everyday Ethics for Business and Life.* Jerusalem, Israel: Ktav, 2003.
Steven H. Miles	*The Hippocratic Oath and the Ethics of Medicine.* New York: Oxford University Press, 2004.
Richard B. Miller	*Children, Ethics, and Modern Medicine.* Bloomington: Indiana University Press, 2003.
Zell Miller	*A Deficit of Decency.* Macon, GA: Stroud & Hall, 2005.

Philip G. Peters Jr.   *How Safe Is Safe Enough? Obligations to the Children of Reproductive Technology.* New York: Oxford University Press, 2004.

David Pritchard   *Holding the Media Accountable: Citizens, Ethics, and the Law.* Bloomington: Indiana University Press, 2000.

Scott B. Rae and Kenman L. Wong, eds.   *Beyond Integrity: A Judeo-Christian Approach to Business Ethics.* 2nd ed. Grand Rapids, MI: Zondervan, 2004.

Ian Richards   *Quagmires and Quandaries: Exploring Journalism Ethics.* Sydney, Australia: University of New South Wales Press, 2005.

Joan Rothschild   *The Dream of the Perfect Child.* Bloomington: Indiana University Press, 2005.

Index